Best of WW

135 of our most
loved recipes for
everyday cooking

WW Healthy Kitchen.

Vice President, Content: Stacey C. Rivera

Global Creative Director: Theron Long

Executive Managing Editor: Amy Grippo

Senior Director of Content Innovation: Jill Herzig

Executive Food Editor: Lisa Chernick

Copy Editor: Christina Doka

Contributing Editors: Jackie Mills, MS, RD; Deborah Mintcheff; Alice Thompson

Recipe Developers: Jackie Mills, MS, RD; Deborah Mintcheff; Eileen Runyan; Alice Thompson

Art Director: Ed Melnitsky

Designers: Lan Yin Bachelis, Arlene Lappen

Production Manager: Alan Biederman

Photo Director: Shawna Kalish

Cover Photographer: Con Poulos

Cover Food Stylist: Christine Albano

Cover Prop Stylist: Megan Hedgpeth

ABOUT WW

WW (formerly Weight Watchers) is a global wellness company and the world's leading commercial weight-management program. We inspire millions of people to adopt healthy habits for real life. Through our engaging digital experience and face-to-face group workshops, members follow our livable and sustainable program that encompasses healthy eating, physical activity, and a helpful mindset. With more than five decades of experience in building communities and our deep expertise in behavioral science, we aim to deliver wellness for all. To learn more about the WW approach to healthy living, please visit WW.com. For more information about our global business, visit our corporate website at corporate.ww.com.

**Sesame chicken,
page 152**

Contents

Eat *your* way

The best pastas? Check. The most-loved chicken recipes? Yep, we've got plenty of those, too, along with iconic holiday desserts, the freshest vegetables, barbecue must-haves, dips and snacks for watching the game, and cozy chilis and stews for chilly nights. In this essential resource, we've collected our tastiest recipes from WW.com, WW magazine, and WW cookbooks. You'll find our best takes on all the seasonal dishes you'd want to make in spring, summer, winter, and fall, plus bonus make-anytime recipes for favorites like mac 'n' cheese, flourless pancakes, stir-fried sesame chicken and broccoli, and two-ingredient-dough pizza, to name just a few. We hope you enjoy making these as much as we do.

Plus, for each recipe, you'll see its SmartPoints® value on each of the three *myWW*™ plans. So whether you're on Green, Blue, or Purple, tracking will be simple. Our science-backed SmartPoints® system at the core of each plan nudges you toward plenty of foods like fruits, vegetables, lean proteins, and healthy fats, while guiding you away from foods high in sugar and unhealthy fats. And no matter which plan you're on, you'll have a personalized amount of SmartPoints to spend on any food you love, along with 100-, 200-, or 300-plus ZeroPoint™ foods that you don't have to measure or track! Each plan is designed to promote equal weight loss, and these simple, time-tested recipes will help make the journey a lot more delicious!

Look for these icons throughout the book to choose the recipes that best fit your needs.

Vegetarian
Recipes that contain no animal-flesh foods or products made from animal flesh, though they may contain eggs and dairy products.

Vegan
Recipes that contain no animal-flesh foods, eggs, dairy products, or honey.

Gluten-free
Recipes that contain no wheat, barley, or rye, or any products that are made from these ingredients.

Dairy-free
Recipes that contain no milk from any animal and no products made from animal milk.

Nut-free
Recipes that contain no tree nuts or peanuts.

No-noodle vegetable
lasagna, page 281

Spring

Open-face egg salad sandwiches

Prep 15 min   No cook   Serves 6

(5) (3) (3)   (🥕)(🚫)

Use Greek yogurt in place of mayo for a welcome tanginess in this salad. To add texture, leave some bigger chunks when chopping the eggs.

⅓   **cup plain low-fat Greek yogurt**

1   **scallion, thinly sliced**

2   **tsp honey mustard**

1   **tsp lemon juice**

1   **tsp minced tarragon**

¼   **tsp salt**

6   **large hard-boiled eggs, peeled and chopped**

6   **slices reduced-calorie whole-wheat bread, toasted**

1½   **cups baby arugula**

½   **avocado, peeled and cut into 12 thin slices**

2   **small radishes, very thinly sliced, for garnish**

Pepper, for seasoning

1 To make egg salad: In a medium bowl, combine yogurt, scallion, honey mustard, lemon juice, tarragon, and salt; gently stir in chopped eggs.

2 Top each toast half with ¼ cup arugula, 2 slices avocado, and ⅓ cup egg salad; garnish with radishes. Season with pepper to taste.

Per serving (1 piece toast with ⅓ cup egg salad): 165 Cal, 9 g Total Fat, 2 g Sat Fat, 246 mg Sod, 13 g Total Carb, 3 g Sugar, 4 g Fib, 11 g Prot.

Deviled eggs with capers and dill

Prep 15 min   No cook   Serves 6

3 **0** **0**

Streamline this recipe's prep by buying peeled hard-cooked eggs at your grocery store.

6   **large hard-boiled eggs, peeled and halved lengthwise**

3   **tbsp plain fat-free Greek yogurt**

1   **tbsp whole-grain Dijon mustard**

¾   **tsp chopped dill, plus more for garnish**

¾   **tsp minced shallot**

⅛   **tsp kosher salt, plus more for garnish**

Pinch black pepper, plus more for garnish

1½ **tsp drained capers**

1 Carefully remove yolks from eggs; place yolks in a small bowl. Add yogurt, mustard, dill, shallot, salt, and pepper; using a fork, mash until smooth.

2 Spoon or pipe yolk mixture into egg white halves. Serve garnished with dill, salt, pepper, and capers.

Per serving (2 filled egg halves): 85 Cal, 5 g Total Fat, 2 g Sat Fat, 179 mg Sod, 1 g Total Carb, 1 g Sugar, 0 g Fib, 7 g Prot.

Spring pea and tofu dip

Prep 12 min   Cook 3 min, plus chilling   Serves 8

Silken tofu gives creamy texture and peas lend body to this dairy-free dip. Scallions and mint are wonderful but dill or tarragon would be, too.

10 oz frozen baby peas or shelled fresh peas

8 oz low-fat silken tofu

1 tbsp extra-virgin olive oil

1½ tsp grated lemon zest

2 tbsp lemon juice

1 tsp salt (or to taste)

¼ tsp coarsely ground black pepper (or to taste)

½ cup firmly packed mint leaves, plus more for garnish

½ cup chopped scallions, plus more for garnish

1 Fill a medium saucepan halfway with water; bring to a boil. Add peas, then return to a boil; boil until peas are crisp-tender, 1 minute. Drain and rinse under cold water until cool; drain again.

2 Put peas into a food processor; add tofu, oil, lemon zest and juice, salt, and pepper. Process until smooth. Add mint and scallions; pulse until herbs are finely chopped.

3 Transfer to a bowl; cover; and refrigerate until chilled, at least 30 minutes or up 2 days. Garnish with additional scallions or mint.

Per serving (¼ cup): 56 Cal, 2 g Total Fat, 1 g Sat Fat, 353 mg Sod, 7 g Total Carb, 2 g Sugar, 2 g Fib, 4 g Prot.

Frisée au lardons salad

Prep 10 min   Cook 10 min   Serves 4

5 **3** **3**

Turkey bacon adds saltiness and smokiness to this French-inspired salad. The rich yolk from the poached egg, together with the dressing, makes this a knockout dish.

8	slices turkey bacon
3	tbsp white-wine vinegar, divided
4	large eggs
1	cup chicken broth
1	tbsp garlic-flavored olive oil
⅛	tsp salt (or to taste)
⅛	tsp black pepper (or to taste)
4	cups chopped frisée

1 In a large skillet over medium-low heat, cook bacon until crisp, about 5 to 6 minutes. (Or cook in microwave according to package directions.) Chop into small pieces.

2 Meanwhile, in a large saucepan over medium-high heat, bring 3 inches water and 1 tbsp vinegar to a boil. Lower heat to keep a simmer. Crack 1 egg into a small cup. Holding cup close to surface of water, slip egg into water. Repeat with remaining eggs. Simmer until egg whites are set and yolks begin to thicken but are not hard, 3 to 4 minutes. Using a slotted spoon, remove eggs from water; set aside.

3 To make dressing: In a medium bowl, whisk together broth, remaining 2 tbsp vinegar, and oil. Season with salt and pepper; stir in bacon.

4 On 4 plates, arrange frisée. Top each with a poached egg and drizzle with about ¼ cup dressing.

Per serving (1 salad): 186 Cal, 14 g Total Fat, 3 g Sat Fat, 695 mg Sod, 3 g Total Carb, 2 g Sugar, 1 g Fib, 12 g Prot.

Easy and perfect poached chicken

Prep 15 min   Cook 30 min   Serves 8

(3) (0) (0)   (※) (※) (※)

A gentle cooking method (think a calm simmer, not a vigorous boil) is the key to tender, succulent poached chicken that can serve as a base for endless healthful meals.

10	**sprigs thyme**
10	**sprigs parsley**
1	**large lemon, quartered, divided**
4	**quarts chicken broth (or water)**
1	**bay leaf**
1	**large stalk celery, thickly sliced**
2	**large shallots, halved**
1	**tsp whole black peppercorns**
1	**tbsp kosher salt**
8	**(6-oz) skinless boneless chicken breasts**

1 Tie thyme and parsley together with kitchen twine. Into a small bowl or cup, squeeze juice from 1 lemon quarter.

2 In a large Dutch oven or large straight-sided skillet, combine herb bundle, remaining lemon, lemon juice, broth (or water), bay leaf, celery, shallots, peppercorns, and salt. Bring to a boil over high heat.

3 Reduce heat to medium and add chicken (if not fully submerged, add boiling water to cover chicken). Watch liquid carefully and adjust heat to maintain liquid so that particles in liquid are moving and surface is steaming but no bubbles rise (do not allow liquid to come to a simmer).

4 Poach chicken until an instant-read thermometer inserted into thickest part reads 165°F, 15 to 20 minutes.

5 Transfer chicken to a large plate; loosely cover and let cool to room temperature. Use immediately or cover and refrigerate up to 4 days.

Per serving (1 chicken breast): 220 Cal, 5 g Total Fat, 1 g Sat Fat, 823 mg Sod, 4 g Total Carb, 1 g Sugar, 1 g Fib, 39 g Prot.

Serving idea
• Slice chicken thinly on bias and top with marinara, part-skim mozzarella, pecorino, and basil; microwave for a quick, easy, healthier chicken parm.
• Shred it and toss with salsa and sliced avocado; put in a wrap with lettuce.
• Shred it and toss into a broth with curry paste, julienned vegetables, and herbs.

Lemony sugar snap pea salad

Prep 15 min   Cook 5 min   Serves 4

3 **3** **3**

Eat this tender salad as soon as you prepare it in order to experience optimal flavor and crunch. You can prep all the ingredients ahead, then toss everything together just before serving.

2 **cups sugar snap peas, trimmed (about 7 oz)**

2 **tbsp lemon juice**

1½ **tbsp olive oil**

¼ **tsp salt (or to taste)**

⅛ **tsp black pepper**

2 **Kirby cucumbers, halved lengthwise and thinly sliced**

¼ **cup crumbled feta**

3 **tbsp chopped chives**

3 **tbsp thinly sliced mint**

1 Bring a large pot of water to a boil. Add snap peas; cook until peas turn bright green and are crisp-tender, about 1 minute. Drain and rinse with cold running water until cool; drain again. Thinly slice peas lengthwise; set aside.

2 In a medium bowl, combine lemon juice, oil, salt, and pepper. Add cooked peas, cucumbers, feta, chives, and mint; gently toss to combine.

Per serving (about 1 cup): 100 Cal, 7 g Total Fat, 2 g Sat Fat, 254 mg Sod, 7 g Total Carb, 3 g Sugar, 2 g Fib, 3 g Prot.

Shaved asparagus salad

Prep 20 min   No cook   Serves 6

2 **2** **2**   ⓥ ⓖ

Ricotta salata is a crumbly cheese with a salty, milky flavor. If you can't find it, crumbled feta or grated Pecorino Romano will give you a similar result.

1   **tbsp chopped capers, plus 2 tsp caper juice**

1   **tbsp white-wine vinegar**

1   **tbsp extra-virgin olive oil**

Grated lemon zest and lemon juice (optional)

2   **lb thick asparagus spears, trimmed**

3   **tbsp pine nuts, toasted, divided**

2   **tbsp chopped parsley**

2   **tbsp chopped chives**

2   **tbsp chopped tarragon**

½   **tsp kosher salt (or to taste)**

¼   **tsp black pepper (or to taste)**

1   **oz ricotta salata**

1 To make dressing: In a medium bowl, combine capers and their juice, vinegar, and oil. Add lemon juice or zest to taste. Set aside.

2 Using a vegetable peeler, shave asparagus into long, thin strips; add to bowl with dressing. Add 1½ tbsp pine nuts, then add parsley, chives, and tarragon; toss to coat. Season with salt and pepper; transfer to a serving platter or bowl.

3 Using a Microplane or the small holes of a box grater, finely grate cheese over top; sprinkle with remaining 1½ tbsp pine nuts.

Per serving (1 cup): 88 Cal, 6 g Total Fat, 1 g Sat Fat, 244 mg Sod, 7 g Total Carb, 3 g Sugar, 3 g Fib, 5 g Prot.

Shopping tip
Choose thick asparagus spears or it will be difficult to shave them into long strips with your vegetable peeler.

Fettuccine with salmon and asparagus

Prep 8 min   Cook 20 min   Serves 4

6 4 4   (icons)

Try this pasta dish with broccolini or even regular broccoli in seasons when asparagus isn't at its prime. The recipe serves 4 as a light first course or 2 as a main.

4   **oz fettuccine**

2   **tsp olive oil**

3   **garlic cloves, finely chopped**

⅛   **tsp red pepper flakes**

½   **lb asparagus, trimmed and cut diagonally into 1-inch pieces**

¼   **tsp plus ⅛ tsp salt, divided**

1   **(6-oz) skinless salmon fillet**

1   **tbsp lemon juice**

1 Cook fettuccine according to package directions; drain and set aside.

2 Meanwhile, in a large skillet over medium-high heat, warm oil. Add garlic and red pepper flakes; cook, stirring constantly, until fragrant, about 1 minute. Add asparagus and cook, stirring constantly, until asparagus is bright green, about 2 minutes. Stir in ¼ cup water and ¼ tsp salt; cover and cook until asparagus is almost tender, about 2 minutes. Uncover and cook until asparagus is tender, about 1 minute. Remove from heat and set aside.

3 In a microwave-safe bowl, sprinkle salmon with lemon juice and remaining ⅛ tsp salt. Cover and microwave on High until salmon is just opaque in center, 2 to 3 minutes. Using a fork, break fillet into bite-size pieces and stir gently to mix with cooking juices in bowl.

4 To skillet with asparagus, add pasta and salmon with cooking juices; toss gently to combine.

Per serving (about ¾ cup): 229 Cal, 8 g Total Fat, 2 g Sat Fat, 247 mg Sod, 25 g Total Carb, 2 g Sugar, 2 g Fib, 14 g Prot.

Pasta and spring vegetables with feta

Prep 30 min   Cook 10 min   Serves 6

(9) (6) (2)   (symbol) (symbol)

Substitute the same amount of shelled edamame if fava beans are hard to find. Limas or broad beans would also work.

½   **lb whole-wheat fusilli**

1½ **cups fresh shelled peeled fava beans (or frozen peeled fava beans, thawed)**

½   **lb asparagus, cut into 1½-inch lengths**

2   **cups grape or cherry tomatoes, halved**

¼   **cup chopped flat-leaf parsley**

2   **tbsp thinly sliced mint leaves**

2   **tbsp extra-virgin olive oil**

½   **tsp grated lemon zest**

2   **tbsp lemon juice**

2   **garlic cloves, minced**

½   **tsp salt**

¼   **tsp black pepper**

¼   **cup crumbled feta**

1 Cook pasta according to package directions, adding fava beans and asparagus during last 2 minutes of cooking time. Drain and rinse under cold running water until cool; drain again.

2 Meanwhile, in large bowl, combine tomatoes, parsley, mint, oil, lemon zest and juice, garlic, salt, and pepper. Add pasta mixture to bowl and toss to coat. Sprinkle with feta.

Per serving (1 cup): 337 Cal, 7 g Total Fat, 2 g Sat Fat, 279 mg Sod, 55 g Total Carb, 4 g Sugar, 15 g Fib, 18 g Prot.

Spaghetti with creamy herb sauce

Prep 15 min   Cook 25 min   Serves 6

Swap the herbs and greens in this silky vegan sauce for whatever you like best or have on hand; spinach and cilantro would be a nice option. In addition to being an excellent pasta sauce, this makes a great dip.

4	**shallots, peeled and left whole**
2	**tsp olive oil**
8	**oz silken tofu (about 1 cup)**
½	**cup watercress, tough stems removed**
¼	**cup flat-leaf parsley leaves**
3	**tbsp lemon juice**
⅛	**tsp salt (or to taste)**
⅛	**tsp black pepper (or to taste)**
9	**cups hot cooked whole-wheat spaghetti**

1 Preheat oven to 450°F.

2 Place shallots on a large sheet of aluminum foil. Bring 4 corners of foil together to make an open pouch. Pour oil over shallots and pinch foil ends together to close pouch; place on a baking sheet. Roast for 25 minutes. Carefully remove pouch from oven, open, and let shallots cool.

3 In a blender or food processor, place tofu, watercress, and parsley and blend on Low for 20 seconds; add lemon juice and roasted shallots. Blend on High for 30 seconds; using a spatula, scrape down sides of container. Season with salt and pepper. Serve over spaghetti.

Per serving (1½ cups spaghetti and ½ cup sauce): 312 Cal, 6 g Total Fat, 1 g Sat Fat, 63 mg Sod, 58 g Total Carb, 4 g Sugar, 8 g Fib, 13 g Prot.

Prep ahead
Sauce can be stored in the refrigerator for up to 5 days.

Potato salad with feta, olives, and dill

Prep 15 min Cook 15 min Serves 6

4 4 2   🥕 🌾 🥛

This Greek-inspired version of a picnic-menu mainstay is creamy, lemony, and delicious.

1½ **lb red baby potatoes, quartered**

⅓ **cup plain low-fat Greek yogurt**

¼ **cup reduced-fat mayonnaise**

2 **tbsp chopped dill**

2 **tsp lemon juice**

1 **tsp Dijon mustard**

1 **tsp kosher salt**

¼ **tsp black pepper**

½ **small red onion, minced**

6 **medium kalamata olives, chopped**

2 **tbsp crumbled feta**

1 In a medium saucepan, place potatoes and enough water to cover; bring to a boil over high heat. Reduce heat to low and simmer until potatoes are fork tender, about 10 minutes; drain and let cool.

2 Meanwhile, to make dressing: In a small bowl, whisk together yogurt, mayonnaise, dill, lemon juice, mustard, salt, and pepper.

3 Place cooled potatoes in a serving bowl; add dressing and onion and toss gently to combine. Sprinkle with olives and feta.

Per serving (about ¾ cup): 137 Cal, 5 g Total Fat, 1 g Sat Fat, 499 mg Sod, 20 g Total Carb, 2 g Sugar, 3 g Fib, 4 g Prot.

Hearty chicken stew with parsley dumplings

Prep 20 min   Cook 55 min   Serves 6

⑨ ⑤ ⑤   ⊗

Fluffy dumplings floating in an herbed chicken-and-vegetable stew is comfort food at its best.

1   tbsp canola oil
1   large onion, coarsely chopped
4   garlic cloves, minced
4   carrots, cut into 1½-inch lengths
3   celery stalks, cut into 1½-inch lengths
4   cups chicken broth
2   thyme sprigs
¾   tsp salt, divided
¼   tsp black pepper
6   (½-lb) bone-in skinless chicken breasts
1   large egg
⅔   cup fat-free milk
2   cups all-purpose flour
1½ tsp baking powder
1   tbsp chopped parsley

1 In a Dutch oven over medium heat, warm oil. Add onion and garlic; cook, stirring occasionally, until onion is softened, about 5 minutes. Stir in carrots, celery, broth, thyme, ¼ tsp salt, and pepper. Add chicken and bring to a boil, skimming off any foam that rises to surface. Reduce heat and simmer until chicken is cooked through, about 30 minutes. Remove and discard thyme sprigs. Transfer chicken to a plate and let cool. Separate meat from bones; discard bones.

2 To make dumplings: In a medium bowl, whisk together egg and milk until frothy. Whisk in 1 cup flour, baking powder, and remaining ½ tsp salt. Add remaining 1 cup flour and parsley, stirring until a thick batter forms.

3 Return broth to a simmer over medium-high heat. Reduce heat to medium. Drop batter by heaping ¼ cupfuls into broth, making a total of 6 dumplings, and cook 7 minutes; carefully turn dumplings over. Cook, covered, until dumplings are light and fluffy, about 7 minutes more.

4 Return chicken to pot and cook until heated through, 3 minutes more.

5 Among 6 large, shallow serving bowls, evenly divide chicken, dumplings, broth, and vegetables.

Per serving (⅙ of chicken and vegetables with broth and 1 dumpling): 507 Cal, 10 g Total Fat, 2 g Sat Fat, 1,161 mg Sod, 42 g Total Carb, 6 g Sugar, 3 g Fib, 60 g Prot.

Lentil, cucumber, and smoked trout salad

Prep 20 min   No cook   Serves 4

(10) (4) (4)

This plate comes together fast, thanks to a couple of smart convenience products: precooked lentils, which you can buy in the supermarket's produce section, and smoked trout, a refrigerated, no-cook protein that's usually found next to the smoked salmon.

1	**cup plain fat-free Greek yogurt**
2	**tbsp tahini**
½	**tsp salt, divided**
1	**small garlic clove, grated**
2	**tbsp finely chopped shallot**
2	**tbsp extra-virgin olive oil**
2	**tbsp red-wine vinegar**
1	**tbsp whole-grain mustard**
¼	**tsp black pepper**
1	**(17.6-oz) package cooked lentils (about 2½ cups)**
2	**cups cherry tomatoes, halved**
2	**Persian (mini) cucumbers, thinly sliced (about 1½ cups)**
2	**tbsp chopped dill**
8	**oz smoked trout, skin removed**

1 In a small bowl, stir together yogurt, tahini, ¼ tsp salt, and garlic until blended. Set aside.

2 To make dressing: In a small jar with a tight-fitting lid, combine shallot, oil, vinegar, mustard, remaining ¼ tsp salt, and pepper; shake well.

3 In a medium bowl, combine lentils and 2½ tbsp dressing; toss to coat. Set aside.

4 In another medium bowl, combine tomatoes, cucumbers, dill, and remaining dressing; toss to coat.

5 Onto each of 4 plates, spoon about ¼ cup yogurt mixture, spreading in an even layer. Top with ⅔ cup lentil mixture, then with ¾ cup tomato mixture. Top evenly with trout. Serve at room temperature.

Per serving (1 plate): 410 Cal, 15 g Total Fat, 3 g Sat Fat, 1,050 mg Sod, 35 g Total Carb, 6 g Sugar, 12 g Fib, 33 g Prot.

Pan-fried fish sandwich

Prep 15 min   Cook 6 min   Serves 4

(7) (6) (6)   (⊗)

Swap in Pecorino Romano for the Parmesan to give the cornmeal crust a sharper bite. If you like to have lettuce leaves that fit the bun just right, Bibb is a great choice.

Olive-oil nonstick spray

¼	cup yellow cornmeal
2	tbsp grated Parmesan
1	tbsp minced fresh thyme (or 1 tsp dried thyme)
½	tsp salt (or to taste)
½	tsp black pepper (or to taste)
4	(4-oz) flounder fillets
1	tbsp Dijon mustard
2	large egg whites, beaten until stiff and placed in a shallow bowl
1	tbsp olive oil
4	tsp tartar sauce, divided
4	light hamburger rolls or buns
½	lemon, cut into 4 wedges
4	lettuce leaves
8	tomato slices

1 In a medium bowl, combine cornmeal, Parmesan, thyme, salt, and pepper; set aside.

2 Spread mustard onto both sides of fish fillets. Dip fish into egg white, turning to coat, then dip into cornmeal mixture, turning to coat.

3 Spray a large ovenproof skillet with nonstick spray and set over medium heat; add oil and warm until hot. Add fish and cook, turning once, until just opaque in center, 4 to 6 minutes.

4 On bottom half of each roll, spread 1 tsp tartar sauce; top each with a fish fillet and lemon juice squeezed from 1 wedge. Top evenly with lettuce and tomato, then with roll tops.

Per serving (1 sandwich): 271 Cal, 8 g Total Fat, 2 g Sat Fat, 990 mg Sod, 29 g Total Carb, 4 g Sugar, 4 g Fib, 21 g Prot.

Grilled tuna with cucumber-noodle salad

Prep 15 min   Cook 15 min   Serves 4

6 5 5

You can leave the skin on these cucumbers. English and Persian varieties have few seeds and skin that's thin and unwaxed.

3	**tbsp lime juice**
2	**tbsp rice vinegar**
1½	**tbsp sugar**
1	**tsp chili-garlic sauce**
½	**tsp salt, divided**
4	**oz thin rice noodles**
6	**radishes, thinly sliced**
½	**English (seedless) cucumber, halved lengthwise, seeded, and sliced**
¼	**medium red onion, thinly sliced**
¼	**cup cilantro leaves, plus more for garnish**
4	**(5-oz) tuna steaks**
1	**tsp olive oil**
½	**tsp black pepper**
½	**lime, cut into 4 wedges**

1 In a medium bowl, combine lime juice, vinegar, sugar, chili-garlic sauce, and ¼ tsp salt. Add ⅓ cup hot water and stir until sugar dissolves. Set aside to cool.

2 Meanwhile, cook rice noodles according to package directions. Rinse with cold water and drain. Add to lime juice mixture. Add radishes, cucumber, onion, and cilantro and toss to combine. Set aside.

3 Heat a ridged grill pan over medium-high heat. Brush tuna with oil; sprinkle with remaining ¼ tsp salt and pepper. Place in pan and cook, turning once, 6 minutes for rare or to desired doneness. Cut steaks across grain into ¼-inch-thick slices. Among 4 plates, evenly divide noodle salad. Top evenly with tuna and garnish with cilantro leaves. Serve with lime wedges.

Per serving (1 tuna steak and 1¼ cups noodle salad): 302 Cal, 2 g Total Fat, 0 g Sat Fat, 410 mg Sod, 33 g Total Carb, 6 g Sugar, 2 g Fib, 36 g Prot.

Salmon with basil-Dijon cream sauce

Prep 10 min   Cook 10 min   Serves 1

(10) (4) (4)

This meal comes together fast and can easily be scaled up to accommodate as many guests as you need it to. Plus, the recipe works just as well with arctic char, tuna, or tilapia.

Nonstick spray

½   **tsp olive oil**

¼   **tsp minced garlic**

½   **tsp minced shallot or red onion**

1 ½ **tsp dry white wine**

1   **tsp Dijon mustard**

¼   **cup skim milk**

1   **tbsp reduced-fat whipped cream cheese**

2   **tbsp thinly sliced basil**

1   **(4-oz) skinless salmon fillet**

⅛   **tsp salt (or to taste)**

⅛   **tsp black pepper (or to taste)**

1 In a small skillet over medium heat, warm oil. Add garlic and shallot; cook, stirring constantly, until shallot starts to soften and edges become slightly brown, 2 to 3 minutes. Add wine, then whisk in mustard. Whisk in milk. Whisk in cream cheese until smooth. Stir in basil and remove from heat; transfer to a small bowl and set aside. Wipe out skillet with paper towels.

2 Sprinkle salmon with salt and pepper. Spray same skillet with nonstick spray; set over medium-high heat. Place salmon in skillet and cook until underside is slightly browned, 2 to 3 minutes. Reduce heat to medium-low and, using a large spatula, flip salmon; cover pan and continue cooking until salmon is just opaque in center, 4 to 5 minutes.

3 Transfer salmon to a plate and serve sauce on the side or drizzled over.

Per serving (1 salmon fillet and about ¼ cup sauce): 326 Cal, 21 g Total Fat, 6 g Sat Fat, 527 mg Sod, 5 g Total Carb, 4 g Sugar, 0 g Fib, 25 g Prot.

Rainbow carrots and sugar snaps

Prep 20 min   Cook 8 min   Serves 6

② ② ②   Ⓥ Ⓖ Ⓓ

Scrub the carrots with a vegetable brush instead of peeling them to preserve more of their nutrients.

¼	cup slivered almonds
2	cups (¼-inch-thick) diagonal slices rainbow carrots
1	cup sugar snap peas, trimmed
¼	cup chopped shallot
2	tbsp chopped dill
1	tbsp olive oil
1	tbsp sherry vinegar or white-wine vinegar
1	garlic clove, peeled and smashed
2	tsp honey
½	tsp salt
¼	tsp black pepper

1 Preheat oven to 350°F.

2 Place almonds on a small baking sheet; bake 5 minutes. Stir almonds and continue baking until just golden, 5 to 8 minutes. Transfer to a small bowl; let cool.

3 Meanwhile, in a medium saucepan over high heat, bring 1 qt water to a boil. Add carrots; cook 1 minute (cook an additional minute if you like them more tender). Add peas; cook until just bright green, 2 minutes. Drain vegetables; rinse under cold water until cool and drain again.

4 In a medium bowl, combine cooked carrots and peas, shallot, dill, oil, vinegar, garlic, honey, salt, and pepper; toss to combine (remove garlic clove, if desired). Sprinkle with reserved almonds.

Per serving (½ cup): 84 Cal, 5 g Total Fat, 1 g Sat Fat, 225 mg Sod, 10 g Total Carb, 5 g Sugar, 3 g Fib, 2 g Prot.

Pork tenderloin with watercress salad

Prep 15 min   Cook 25 min   Serves 4

Choose tomatoes in a variety of colors for a pretty presentation. Also, feel free to swap the watercress for baby arugula or a different green, if you'd prefer.

2	garlic cloves, minced, divided
2	tsp chili powder
1	tsp ground cumin
½	tsp ground coriander
½	tsp salt, divided
½	tsp black pepper, divided
1	lb lean pork tenderloin, trimmed
1	tsp canola oil
2	tbsp orange juice
2	tbsp lime juice
1	scallion, minced
1½	tbsp olive oil
1	tbsp lemon juice
1	tsp sugar
6	cups watercress
1	cup grape or cherry tomatoes, halved

1 Preheat oven to 425°F.

2 To make pork, in a small bowl, combine 1 garlic clove, chili powder, cumin, coriander, ¼ tsp salt, and ¼ tsp pepper. Rub seasoning all over pork.

3 In a large ovenproof skillet over medium-high heat, warm canola oil. Add tenderloin and cook, turning occasionally, until browned on all sides, about 8 minutes. Transfer skillet to oven and roast until an instant-read thermometer inserted into center of meat registers 145°F, about 15 minutes. Let rest 5 minutes, then cut into 24 slices.

4 Meanwhile, to make dressing: In a small bowl, whisk together orange juice, lime juice, scallion, olive oil, lemon juice, sugar, remaining garlic clove, remaining ¼ tsp salt, and remaining ¼ tsp pepper.

5 Arrange watercress and tomatoes on a platter. Top with slices of tenderloin and drizzle with dressing.

Per serving (6 slices pork, 1¼ cups salad, and 2 tbsp dressing): 211 Cal, 9 g Total Fat, 1 g Sat Fat, 414 mg Sod, 7 g Total Carb, 3 g Sugar, 1 g Fib, 26 g Prot.

Lamb chops with balsamic tomatoes

Prep 5 min   Cook 15 min   Serves 4

4 4 4   (icons)

These balsamic tomatoes are an excellent quick side dish. Serve them with other main dishes, including roasted salmon or grilled chicken.

2	tsp olive oil, divided
4	(4-oz) lean bone-in lamb chops, trimmed (about 1¼-inches thick)
2	tbsp chopped rosemary
¾	tsp salt, divided
¼	tsp black pepper, divided
2	cups cherry tomatoes
2	scallions, thinly sliced
2	tbsp balsamic vinegar

1 In a large skillet over medium-high heat, warm 1 tsp oil.

2 Sprinkle lamb with rosemary, ½ tsp salt, and ⅛ tsp pepper. Place lamb in skillet and cook, turning once, until an instant read thermometer inserted into sides of chops registers 145°F, about 10 minutes. Transfer lamb to a plate and keep warm.

3 Reduce heat to medium and add remaining 1 tsp oil to skillet. Add tomatoes and scallions and cook, stirring often, until tomatoes are just softened, about 2 minutes. Add vinegar, remaining ¼ tsp salt, and remaining ⅛ tsp pepper and cook 30 seconds. Serve lamb with tomatoes.

Per serving (1 lamb chop and ½ cup tomatoes): 207 Cal, 9 g Total Fat, 3 g Sat Fat, 520 mg Sod, 5 g Total Carb, 3 g Sugar, 1 g Fib, 25 g Prot.

Roasted chicken, artichokes, and potatoes

Prep 25 min   Cook 1 hr 20 min   Serves 6

5 **5** **3**   ⊘ ⊘ ⊘

If you can't find baby artichokes, frozen artichoke hearts are a good substitute. They won't look as lovely, but the taste will be the same.

Olive-oil nonstick spray
1	**(3½-lb) whole chicken**
2	**garlic cloves, minced**
2	**tsp minced thyme**
3	**tsp grated lemon zest, divided**
1	**tsp olive oil**
¾	**tsp salt, divided**
½	**tsp black pepper**
1½	**lb baby or fingerling potatoes, halved or quartered if large**
4	**tbsp lemon juice, divided**
1	**lb baby artichokes**

1 Preheat oven to 400°F.

2 Remove and discard giblets and any large pieces of fat from chicken. If desired, fold wing tips under first joint and tie legs together with kitchen string. Loosen skin from breast and drumsticks by easing fingers under skin and gently separating skin from meat.

3 In a small bowl, combine garlic, thyme, 1 tsp lemon zest, oil, ½ tsp of salt, and pepper. Rub half of mixture under loosened skin and over breasts and legs of chicken. Place chicken in a large roasting pan.

4 In a medium bowl, combine potatoes and remaining garlic mixture; toss to coat. Arrange potatoes around chicken in pan.

5 In a large bowl, combine ½ cup water and 2 tbsp lemon juice. Pull tough outer leaves from artichokes and trim stems. Cut about ½ inch off each artichoke top. Cut each artichoke lengthwise in half and dip into lemon water to prevent browning. Place artichoke halves around chicken and drizzle with remaining lemon water. Spray vegetables with nonstick spray.

6 Roast chicken and vegetables, stirring vegetables twice and adding ¼ cup water each time, until an instant-read thermometer inserted into thigh (not touching bone) registers 165°F, about 1 hour 20 minutes. Transfer vegetables to large bowl when tender, after about 1 hour. Add remaining 2 tbsp lemon juice, remaining 2 tsp lemon zest, and remaining ¼ tsp salt to vegetables and toss to coat. Cover to keep warm.

7 Place chicken on a cutting board or work surface. Cover loosely with foil and let stand 10 minutes. Carve chicken and divide chicken and vegetables evenly among 6 plates. Remove chicken skin before eating.

Per serving (⅙ of chicken, 4 artichoke halves, and ¾ cup potatoes): 284 Cal, 5 g Total Fat, 1 g Sat Fat, 483 mg Sod, 27 g Total Carb, 2 g Sugar, 7 g Fib, 33 g Prot.

Grilled lemon chicken with spring peas

Prep 10 min   Cook 10 min   Serves 1

4 **1** **1**   (symbols)

Try pea shoots as a garnish, if your grocery store stocks them. Their slightly sweet earthiness and crunch complement this dish nicely.

Nonstick spray

½   **small lemon**

¾   **tsp Dijon mustard or horseradish mustard**

1   **garlic clove, minced**

5   **oz skinless boneless chicken breast**

½   **tsp olive oil**

¼   **lb snow peas, trimmed**

⅓   **cup thawed frozen green peas**

⅛   **tsp salt**

⅛   **tsp black pepper**

2   **tsp snipped chives (optional)**

1 Grate zest from lemon. In a small shallow dish, stir together lemon zest, mustard, and garlic. Add chicken and turn to coat. Spray a ridged cast-iron grill pan with nonstick spray and set over medium heat. Add chicken and lemon, cut-side down. Cook, turning once, until chicken is cooked through and lemon is well charred, about 8 minutes.

2 Meanwhile, in a medium nonstick skillet over medium heat, warm oil. Add snow peas, green peas, salt, and pepper. Cook, stirring often, until snow peas are crisp-tender, about 2 minutes.

3 Cut lemon into wedges. Transfer pea mixture to a plate and top with chicken. Sprinkle chicken with chives, if desired, and serve with lemon.

Per serving (1 chicken breast, 1⅔ cup peas, and ½ lemon): 295 Cal, 7 g Total Fat, 1 g Sat Fat, 494 mg Sod, 20 g Total Carb, 8 g Sugar, 7 g Fib, 38 g Prot.

Yogurt with rhubarb-raspberry spoon fruit

Prep 10 min   Cook 15 min   Serves 12

Bring home extra rhubarb to prep, chop, and freeze when it's at its peak at the market, and you can revisit this recipe any time of year.

¼ cup granulated sugar

¼ cup packed light brown sugar

1 lb rhubarb, trimmed and thinly sliced, or 1 (10-oz) box frozen sliced rhubarb, thawed

¾ cup raspberries (6 oz)

6 cups plain fat-free Greek yogurt

6 tbsp sliced almonds, toasted

1 In a medium saucepan, combine ½ cup water and both sugars and set over medium-high heat. Cook, stirring frequently, until sugar dissolves, about 2 minutes.

2 Add rhubarb and cook, stirring often, until just tender, 5 to 7 minutes. Add raspberries and cook, stirring often, until berries begin to just fall apart, about 3 minutes. Transfer to a bowl and let cool to room temperature. (The sauce can be made up to 4 days ahead and stored in a covered container in refrigerator.)

3 For each serving, place ½ cup yogurt in bowl. Top with 2 tbsp sauce and ½ tbsp almonds.

Per serving (1 bowl): 129 Cal, 2 g Total Fat, 0 g Sat Fat, 44 mg Sod, 16 g Total Carb, 13 g Sugar, 2 g Fib, 13 g Prot.

Chocolate-berry pavlova

Prep 35 min   Cook 1 hr 30 min, plus cooling   Serves 12

(8) (8) (8)   (🥕) (🌾) (%)

Top this showstopping dessert with any berries you'd like. We suggest choosing whichever ones look the best and taste the sweetest at the market.

4	**large egg whites, at room temperature**
¼	**tsp cream of tartar**
⅛	**tsp salt**
1	**cup superfine sugar**
¼	**cup unsweetened cocoa powder**
½	**cup mascarpone**
4	**oz light cream cheese (Neufchâtel), softened**
1½	**tbsp granulated sugar**
1	**tbsp low-fat (1%) milk**
½	**tsp vanilla extract**
½	**lb strawberries, hulled and sliced (or other berries)**
1	**oz bittersweet chocolate**

1 Preheat oven to 250°F. Line a large baking sheet with parchment paper.

2 To make meringue: In a large bowl, using an electric mixer on medium speed, beat egg whites, cream of tartar, and salt until soft peaks form when beaters are lifted. Add superfine sugar, 2 tbsp at a time, beating until stiff, glossy peaks form.

3 Sift cocoa over beaten whites in 3 additions, using a rubber spatula to gently fold until cocoa is just incorporated, being careful not to deflate meringue. Spoon meringue onto prepared baking sheet and spread to form 9-inch nest with 1-inch-high edge.

4 Bake meringue 1½ hours. Turn oven off and let meringue cool in oven 2 hours. Remove from oven and slide meringue with parchment onto a wire rack and let cool completely.

5 To make filling: In a medium bowl, using an electric mixer on medium speed, beat together mascarpone, cream cheese, granulated sugar, milk, and vanilla until smooth.

6 Transfer meringue to a serving plate. Spoon mascarpone mixture into center of meringue and top with strawberries. Using a vegetable peeler, shave chocolate over berries. Using a serrated knife, cut pavlova into 12 wedges and serve immediately.

Per serving (1 wedge): 160 Cal, 7 g Total Fat, 5 g Sat Fat, 94 mg Sod, 23 g Total Carb, 20 g Sugar, 1 g Fib, 3 g Prot.

Lemon angel food cake with strawberry-balsamic compote

Prep 30 min   Cook 30 min, plus cooling   Serves 16

④ ④ ④   ⊕ ⊘ ⊛

Taste your strawberries before making the compote. If they're at peak-season sweetness, you may opt to use less sugar in the sauce.

1	**cup plus 1 tbsp sugar, divided**
2	**tsp grated lemon zest**
12	**large egg whites, at room temperature**
¼	**tsp salt**
1	**tbsp lemon juice**
1	**tsp vanilla extract**
¾	**tsp cream of tartar**
1	**cup cake flour**
1½	**lb strawberries, hulled and quartered**
1	**tbsp store-bought balsamic glaze**

1 Preheat oven to 350°F.

2 In a small bowl, stir together 1 cup sugar and lemon zest. In a large bowl, using an electric mixer on medium speed, beat egg whites and salt until foamy. Beat in lemon juice and vanilla. Add cream of tartar; beat until soft peaks form when beaters are lifted. Add sugar-lemon mixture, a few tbsp at a time, to egg-white mixture, beating until stiff peaks form. (If lemon zest sticks to beaters, scrape it down to incorporate.)

3 Using a rubber spatula, fold in flour, ¼ cup at a time. (Be careful not to overmix.)

4 Pour batter into an ungreased 10-inch tube pan, spreading evenly. Bake until cake springs back when lightly pressed, 20 to 25 minutes. Invert pan onto its legs or the neck of a bottle and let cool completely.

5 Run a thin knife around edge of cake to loosen it from side and center tube of pan. Remove cake from pan and place on a serving plate.

6 To make compote: In a large bowl, combine ½ lb strawberries and remaining 1 tbsp sugar; using a large spoon or potato masher, coarsely crush strawberries. Stir in remaining strawberries and balsamic glaze.

7 Cut cake into 16 slices and place on plates. Spoon compote evenly over each slice.

Per serving (¹⁄₁₆ of cake and ¼ cup compote): 112 Cal, 0 g Total Fat, 0 g Sat Fat, 78 mg Sod, 24 g Total Carb, 16 g Sugar, 1 g Fib, 4 g Prot.

Blueberry and Meyer lemon sorbet with thyme

Prep 15 min   Cook 8 min, plus chilling and freezing   Serves 8

Meyer lemons are sweeter and less acidic than standard lemons, like a cross between a lemon and a mandarin orange. They're great in dessert recipes, thanks to their natural sweetness.

½   **cup sugar**

8   **thyme sprigs, plus more for garnish**

⅔   **cup lemon juice (from 5 to 6 Meyer lemons)**

3   **cups unsweetened frozen blueberries**

1   **tsp grated lemon zest (optional)**

1 In a small saucepan, combine ⅔ cup water, sugar, and thyme sprigs; set over high heat and bring to a boil. Reduce heat to medium; simmer 5 minutes. Let cool, then refrigerate until chilled, about 1 hour.

2 Remove and discard thyme sprigs. Into a blender, pour chilled sugar mixture, lemon juice, and frozen blueberries; puree until smooth. Transfer mixture to an ice-cream maker and freeze according to manufacturer's instructions. Transfer to airtight container; freeze until firm, at least 2 hours. Garnish each serving with thyme sprigs and lemon zest, if desired.

Per serving (½ cup): 85 Cal, 0 g Total Fat, 0 g Sat Fat, 1 mg Sod, 22 g Total Carb, 18 g Sugar, 2 g Fib, 0 g Prot.

Summer

Pan-fried green tomatoes with remoulade

Prep 5 min   Cook 8 min   Serves 4

2 2 2   🥕 🌾 🍯

Bring Cajun spice to this classic French sauce by adding a little Creole seasoning. This side dish will be a big hit all summer long.

2   **tbsp reduced-fat mayonnaise**

2   **tbsp plain fat-free Greek yogurt**

½   **tsp Dijon mustard**

½   **tsp Creole seasoning**

4   **green tomatoes, cut into ½-inch slices**

¼   **tsp salt**

⅛   **tsp black pepper**

4   **tsp canola oil**

1 To make remoulade: In a small bowl, stir together mayonnaise, yogurt, mustard, and Creole seasoning. Set aside.

2 Sprinkle tomatoes with salt and pepper. In a large heavy skillet over medium-high heat, warm 2 tsp of oil. Add half of tomatoes and cook, turning once, until lightly browned, about 4 minutes. Transfer to a platter and keep warm. Repeat with remaining oil and tomatoes. Serve tomatoes topped with remoulade.

Per serving (3 tomato slices and 1 tbsp remoulade): 91 Cal, 6 g Total Fat, 1 g Sat Fat, 332 mg Sod, 7 g Total Carb, 5 g Sugar, 1 g Fib, 2 g Prot.

Grilled shrimp with Spanish vinaigrette

Prep 35 min   Cook 6 min   Serves 8

② ① ①   Ⓥ Ⓓ Ⓝ

You can skewer the shrimp before grilling to make them easier to turn and serve. Instead of drizzling the vinaigrette, you could place it alongside the shrimp as a dip.

Nonstick spray

2   **tbsp olive oil, divided**

1½ **tbsp lemon juice**

1   **tsp granulated garlic**

½   **tsp kosher salt, plus a pinch**

2   **lb medium shrimp, peeled and deveined**

1   **cup water-packed roasted red peppers, drained**

2   **tsp sherry vinegar**

1   **tsp minced garlic**

¼   **tsp black pepper**

1   **tsp smoked paprika**

½   **tsp ground cumin**

½   **tsp minced oregano**

1 To make shrimp: In a large bowl, stir together 1 tbsp oil, lemon juice, granulated garlic, and a pinch of salt; add shrimp and toss to coat. Let stand at room temperature for 30 minutes.

2 Meanwhile, to make dressing: In a food processor or blender, combine red peppers, remaining 1 tbsp oil, vinegar, minced garlic, remaining ½ tsp salt, black pepper, paprika, cumin, and oregano; puree and set aside.

3 Spray a ridged grill pan with nonstick spray and set over high heat until hot. Place shrimp in pan and grill, turning once, until just opaque throughout, 4 to 6 minutes.

4 Serve shrimp drizzled with dressing.

Per serving (¼ lb shrimp and 2 tbsp dressing): 129 Cal, 5 g Total Fat, 1 g Sat Fat, 887 mg Sod, 7 g Total Carb, 2 g Sugar, 0 g Fib, 16 g Prot.

Fresh corn and black bean salsa

Prep 15 min   No cook   Serves 1

3 0 0

Swap in defrosted frozen corn if you can't find fresh corn at optimal sweetness.

½   **cup fresh corn kernels**

8   **grape tomatoes, quartered**

¼   **cup canned black beans, rinsed and drained**

1   **small scallion, thinly sliced**

2   **tbsp chopped cilantro**

¼   **tsp grated lime zest**

2   **tsp lime juice (or to taste)**

Pinch salt

⅛   **tsp hot pepper sauce (or to taste)**

6   **mini bell peppers, halved and seeded**

1 In a medium bowl, combine corn, tomatoes, beans, scallion, cilantro, lime zest and juice, salt, and pepper sauce.

2 Serve with mini peppers for scopping up salsa.

Per serving (about 1 cup salsa and 6 mini bell peppers): 201 Cal, 2 g Total Fat, 0 g Sat Fat, 553 mg Sod, 43 g Total Carb, 15 g Sugar, 12 g Fib, 9 g Prot.

Layered Southern dip

Prep 30 min No cook Serves 16

1 1 1

Ready for a new take on a favorite party dish? This version of the famous dip makes the most of scallions, bacon, and low-fat dairy.

⅔   **cup chopped bell pepper**

⅔   **cup chopped celery**

⅔   **cup chopped plum tomato**

½   **cup frozen corn kernels, thawed**

¼   **cup finely chopped red onion**

1   **garlic clove, finely chopped**

1   **tsp red-wine vinegar**

1   **tsp extra-virgin olive oil**

½   **tsp black pepper, divided**

¼   **tsp salt, divided**

½   **cup roasted red pepper (packed in water), drained and finely chopped**

½   **cup plain low-fat Greek yogurt**

¼   **cup light cream cheese (Neufchâtel), softened**

2   **scallions, white parts finely chopped and green parts chopped, divided**

¼   **tsp smoked paprika**

1   **cup reduced-fat Mexican blend shredded cheese**

3   **slices turkey bacon, cooked until crisp, crumbled**

1 In a large bowl, combine bell pepper, celery, tomato, corn, onion, garlic, vinegar, oil, ¼ tsp black pepper, and ⅛ tsp salt; set aside to allow flavors to blend.

2 In another large bowl, stir together roasted peppers, yogurt, cream cheese, scallion whites, paprika, remaining ¼ tsp black pepper, and remaining ⅛ tsp salt; mash slightly with a fork.

3 Over the bottom of a 9-inch glass or ceramic pie plate, spread roasted pepper mixture in an even layer; sprinkle with shredded cheese. Spoon vegetable mixture over top; sprinkle with bacon and scallion greens.

Per serving (⅓ cup): 49 Cal, 2 g Total Fat, 1 g Sat Fat, 151 mg Sod, 4 g Total Carb, 2 g Sugar, 1 g Fib, 3 g Prot.

Lemony coleslaw with apples

Prep 15 min   Chill 30 min   Serves 12

This slaw has a bright lemony dressing. Give it even more character by tossing in some chopped dill or mint, and poppy seeds.

½   cup reduced-calorie mayonnaise

¼   cup plain fat-free Greek yogurt

1   tsp grated lemon zest

3   tbsp lemon juice

1   tsp sugar

½   tsp salt

½   tsp black pepper

1   (14-oz) package coleslaw mix (shredded cabbage and carrots)

2   Gala apples, cut into matchsticks

¼   cups chopped flat-leaf parsley

2   scallions, thinly sliced

1 In a medium bowl, whisk together mayonnaise, yogurt, lemon zest, lemon juice, sugar, salt, and pepper. Add coleslaw mix, apples, parsley, and scallions; toss to coat. Cover and chill 30 minutes for flavors to blend.

Per serving (⅔ cup): 65 Cal, 3 g Total Fat, 0 g Sat Fat, 181 mg Sod, 8 g Total Carb, 5 g Sugar, 2 g Fib, 1 g Prot.

Egg salad with cucumber, tomato, and capers

Prep 20 min   No cook   Serves 8

2 **0** **0**

Need a quick and delicious no-cook dinner? Wrap this salad in tender Bibb lettuce leaves or pile it on toast.

½   **cup plain fat-free Greek yogurt**

1   **tbsp minced dill**

1   **tbsp capers, drained and chopped**

1   **tbsp minced shallot**

1½ **tsp Dijon mustard**

½   **tsp kosher salt**

⅛   **tsp black pepper**

6   **large hard-boiled eggs, peeled**

1   **cup grape tomatoes, halved**

1   **cup seeded and diced English cucumber**

¼   **cup thinly sliced scallion, plus more for garnish**

1 In a small bowl, whisk together yogurt, dill, capers, shallot, mustard, salt, and pepper.

2 Cut eggs into large chunks and place in a large bowl; add tomatoes, cucumber, and scallion. Add yogurt mixture to egg mixture and toss to just coat; garnish with scallion.

Per serving (½ cup): 75 Cal, 4 g Total Fat, 1 g Sat Fat, 221 mg Sod, 3 g Total Carb, 2 g Sugar, 0 g Fib, 7 g Prot.

No-mayo pasta e ceci salad

Prep 20 min   Cook 10 min   Serves 8

(8) (4) (4)   (🥕)(🌱)(🚫)(🍫)

Make this your new picnic staple when you need a break from mayo-based salads. It's packed with greens, pasta, and chickpeas (*ceci* in Italian).

6	oz pasta (such as cellentani or campanelle)
3	tbsp extra-virgin olive oil
1	garlic clove, chopped
½	tsp flaky sea salt, divided
1	tsp finely chopped rosemary
½	tsp crushed red pepper flakes (or to taste)
2	(15-oz) cans chickpeas, rinsed and drained
3	packed cups very thinly sliced kale
2	tbsp chopped basil
1	tsp grated lemon zest, plus more for garnish
⅛	tsp black pepper (or to taste)

1 Cook pasta according to package directions; drain, but do not rinse. Transfer pasta to a large plate or large rimmed baking sheet; let cool to room temperature, about 10 minutes.

2 Meanwhile, in a small saucepan, heat oil over very low heat until it begins to just shimmer, about 1 minute; remove from heat. On a cutting board, use the blade and flat side of a chef's knife to chop and smash garlic with ¼ tsp salt to form a paste. Stir garlic paste, rosemary, and red pepper flakes into warm oil.

3 In a large bowl, gently toss together pasta, oil mixture, chickpeas, kale, basil, lemon zest, remaining ¼ tsp salt, and black pepper. Sprinkle with additional lemon zest and red pepper flakes, if desired.

Per serving (1 cup): 274 Cal, 8 g Total Fat, 1 g Sat Fat, 381 mg Sod, 40 g Total Carb, 5 g Sugar, 8 g Fib, 11 g Prot.

Italian pasta salad with tomatoes and artichokes

Prep 18 min   Cook 10 min   Serves 6

Choose the ripest, juiciest tomatoes you can find. Their juices will enhance the dressing. Add grilled chicken or shrimp to turn this into a main course.

1	**lb ripe beefsteak or Campari tomatoes, chopped**
2	**small yellow and orange bell peppers, diced**
1	**(14-oz) can artichoke hearts, drained and coarsely chopped**
1	**cup basil, coarsely chopped**
2	**tbsp red-wine vinegar**
2	**tbsp extra-virgin olive oil**
½	**tsp salt**
½	**tsp black pepper**
¼	**tsp garlic powder (or to taste)**
6	**oz cellentani (aka cavatappi) pasta (about 2 cups)**
⅓	**cup shaved or shredded Parmesan**

1 In a large bowl, combine tomatoes, peppers, artichoke hearts, basil, vinegar, oil, salt, pepper, and garlic powder; toss to combine. Let stand, tossing occasionally, while preparing pasta.

2 Cook pasta according to package directions; drain and rinse with cold water until cool, then drain again.

3 Add pasta to tomato mixture; toss to coat. Add all but 2 tbsp Parmesan; toss again. Sprinkle with remaining Parmesan.

Per serving (1⅓ cups): 204 Cal, 6 g Total Fat, 1 g Sat Fat, 467 mg Sod, 31 g Total Carb, 4 g Sugar, 5 g Fib, 8 g Prot.

Grilled Caesar salad with cherry tomatoes

Prep 12 min Cook 10 min Serves 4

④ ④ ④

Add unexpected smokiness to this salad by giving the lettuce a quick turn on the grill. If you see Little Gem lettuces, buy them. They're a cross between romaine and Bibb, and their compact size makes them easy to grill.

Olive-oil nonstick spray

1	**garlic clove**
3	**tbsp grated Parmesan, divided**
2	**tbsp reduced-fat mayonnaise**
2	**anchovy fillets, drained and patted dry with paper towels**
1	**tbsp lemon juice**
1	**tbsp white balsamic vinegar**
1	**tsp Worcestershire sauce**
½	**tsp Dijon mustard**
½	**tsp agave nectar or honey**
⅛	**tsp black pepper**
4	**romaine lettuce hearts**
4	**(1-oz) slices whole-wheat Italian bread**
¼	**tsp salt**
2	**cups cherry tomatoes, halved**

1 Spray grill rack with nonstick spray. Preheat grill to medium-high or prepare medium-high fire.

2 To make dressing: Place garlic in a mini food processor and pulse until minced. Add 1 tbsp Parmesan, mayonnaise, anchovies, lemon juice, vinegar, Worcestershire, mustard, agave nectar, and pepper; puree. Set aside.

3 Cut each romaine heart lengthwise in half (or into quarters if large), leaving cores intact. Pat dry with paper towels. Lightly spray romaine and bread with olive-oil nonstick spray. Sprinkle romaine with salt.

4 Put romaine on grill rack and grill, turning once, until lightly charred but not limp, about 5 minutes. Place bread on grill rack and grill, turning once, until lightly charred, about 4 minutes. Cut bread into ½-inch cubes.

5 Arrange romaine evenly on 4 plates. Top with bread cubes and tomatoes. Drizzle evenly with dressing and sprinkle with remaining 2 tbsp Parmesan. Serve at once.

Per serving (1 salad): 251 Cal, 7 g Total Fat, 1 g Sat Fat, 574 mg Sod, 39 g Total Carb, 13 g Sugar, 16 g Fib, 14 g Prot.

Grilled corn, chicken, and vegetable salad

Prep 30 min   Cook 25 min, plus chilling   Serves 4

8 5 5   ⊗ ⊘ ⊗

You can serve the salad in sections, as we did here, so everyone can choose the items they like, or toss it all together. It'll be a hit either way.

Nonstick spray

4½ tbsp reduced-sodium chicken broth

¼   cup finely chopped shallot

3   tbsp extra-virgin olive oil

2   tbsp red-wine vinegar

1   tbsp Dijon mustard

1   tbsp chopped oregano

1½ tsp kosher salt, divided, plus more for seasoning

½   tsp black pepper, divided, plus more for seasoning

1   lb skinless boneless chicken breasts

2   large ears corn, husked

1   small yellow bell pepper, quartered

1   small orange bell pepper, quartered

1   small zucchini, halved lengthwise

1   small ripe but firm Hass avocado, halved, pitted, and peeled

1½ cups grape tomatoes or pear tomatoes, halved

½   cup basil leaves

1 To make dressing: In a small bowl, stir together broth, shallots, oil, vinegar, mustard, oregano, ½ tsp salt, and ¼ tsp pepper.

2 Place chicken on a large plate; drizzle with 2 tbsp dressing and turn to coat. Cover and refrigerate at least 20 minutes or up to 2 hours.

3 Meanwhile, spray grill rack with nonstick spray. Preheat grill to medium-high or prepare medium-high fire.

4 Spray chicken, corn, bell peppers, zucchini, and avocado with nonstick spray; sprinkle with remaining 1 tsp salt and remaining ¼ tsp pepper.

5 Place chicken, corn, peppers, and zucchini on grill rack and grill, turning occasionally, until chicken is cooked through and vegetables are lightly charred and tender, 10 to 15 minutes. Place avocado on grill rack and grill, turning once, until grill marks appear, about 2 minutes.

6 Slice chicken, cut corn from cobs (or cut cobs into small pieces), slice peppers, cut zucchini into bite-size chunks, and slice avocado.

7 On a large serving platter, arrange chicken, grilled vegetables, and tomatoes. Drizzle with remaining dressing; sprinkle with basil. Season with more salt and pepper, if desired.

Per serving (¼ of chicken and vegetables and 2½ tbsp dressing): 383 Cal, 20 g Total Fat, 3 g Sat Fat, 906 mg Sod, 23 g Total Carb, 7 g Sugar, 6 g Fib, 30 g Prot.

Mahi mahi soft tacos

Prep 12 min   Cook 13 min, plus chilling   Serves 4

(5) (4) (4)

If you can't find mahi mahi, try swordfish or halibut for a similar texture. But really, any fish will taste great in this marinade!

1	**lb mahi mahi fillets**
½	**tsp salt (or to taste)**
1½	**tbsp minced peeled ginger**
⅓	**cup lime juice**
½	**tbsp packed dark brown sugar**
2	**tbsp minced scallion**
¼	**cup minced cilantro**
8	**(6-inch) corn tortillas, lightly toasted**
2	**cups shredded lettuce**
½	**cup peach or mango salsa**
1	**lime, cut into 4 wedges**

1 Sprinkle fish with salt. In a glass or ceramic medium baking dish, combine ginger, lime juice, sugar, scallion, and cilantro; stir well. Add fish; turn to coat. Cover and refrigerate 20 to 30 minutes.

2 Line broiler rack with foil; preheat broiler.

3 Remove fish from marinade and place on broiler rack; brush with half of marinade. Broil 4 inches from heat for 6 minutes; turn fish and brush with remaining marinade. Broil until fish is just opaque throughout, 5 to 7 minutes, depending on thickness of fish. Cut fish into 8 pieces.

4 Divide fish, lettuce, and salsa evenly among tortillas; fold in half and serve with lime wedges.

Per serving (2 tacos): 242 Cal, 3 g Total Fat, 0 g Sat Fat, 676 mg Sod, 32 g Total Carb, 5 g Sugar, 4 g Fib, 25 g Prot.

Summer vegetable tart

Prep 20 min   Cook 40 min   Serves 8

5 5 5

Show off the season's best tomatoes, zucchini, and summer squash in this eye-catching and tasty recipe. It relies on ready-to-bake frozen pie crust to cut down on prep time.

Nonstick spray

1   **(6-oz) ready-to-bake frozen pie crust, thawed**
2   **large tomatoes, sliced**
1   **large zucchini, sliced**
1   **small yellow summer squash, sliced**
1   **cup part-skim ricotta**
¼   **tsp dried thyme**
¼   **tsp dried basil**
¼   **tsp dried rosemary**
¼   **tsp salt (or to taste)**
⅛   **tsp black pepper (or to taste)**

1 Roll out crust and fit into a 9-inch tart pan; bake according to package directions. Let cool.

2 Adjust oven temperature to 375°F. Spray a large rimmed baking sheet with nonstick spray.

3 Place tomatoes, zucchini, and squash on prepared baking sheet and spray lightly with nonstick spray. Bake until tomatoes are slightly dry and zucchini and squash slices are tender, 20 to 30 minutes; transfer to a large shallow bowl and let cool. Maintain oven temperature.

4 In a small bowl, stir together ricotta, thyme, basil, rosemary, salt, and pepper; spread mixture evenly over crust. Starting at center of crust and working outward, arrange slightly overlapping, alternating rings of vegetables until crust is completely covered.

5 Place tart pan on a baking sheet and bake until heated through, 5 to 10 minutes. Cut into 8 wedges.

Per serving (1 wedge): 155 Cal, 8 g Total Fat, 3 g Sat Fat, 194 mg Sod, 15 g Total Carb, 3 g Sugar, 2 g Fib, 6 g Prot.

Tomato, feta, and fresh herb tart

Prep 20 min   Cook 12 min, plus cooling   Serves 8

2 **2** **2**

You can use any colorful ripe tomatoes in this summer-fresh tart. Even better, include a mix of sizes, too. And if you have a big handful of fresh herbs to use from the garden, no need to stop at 2 tbsp!

Nonstick spray

- **5** **(13 x 18-inch) sheets frozen phyllo dough, thawed**
- **1** **tsp flaky sea salt (such as Maldon), plus a pinch**
- **¼** **tsp black pepper, plus a pinch**
- **7** **tbsp crumbled feta, divided**
- **2** **cups mixed-color cherry tomatoes, each cut crosswise into 3 slices**
- **3** **heirloom or regular tomatoes, cut into ⅛-inch slices**
- **2** **tbsp coarsely chopped basil, chives, tarragon, and/or mint**

1 Position oven rack in middle of oven. Preheat oven to 350°F. Spray a 13 x 18-inch rimmed baking sheet with nonstick spray.

2 Place 1 sheet phyllo on prepared pan; lightly spray with nonstick spray and, using a pastry brush, gently brush so spray coats entire piece of dough. Repeat with remaining phyllo and nonstick spray to make 5 layers. Fold edges over to make a thin rolled rim.

3 Sprinkle a generous pinch of salt and pinch of pepper over phyllo; sprinkle with 3 tbsp feta. Bake until lightly golden, pressing down on dough halfway through cooking, 10 to 12 minutes. Remove from oven; let cool completely on pan, 10 to 15 minutes.

4 Using a large metal spatula, carefully lift and slide cooled crust onto a large cutting board; top with an even layer of tomatoes. Season with salt and pepper (or to taste); scatter remaining feta and herbs over top. Cut into 8 pieces; serve immediately.

Per serving (1 piece): 76 Cal, 3 g Total Fat, 1 g Sat Fat, 389 mg Sod, 10 g Total Carb, 2 g Sugar, 1 g Fib, 3 g Prot.

Zucchini and tomato pita pizzas

Prep 10 min   Cook 6 min   Serves 4

4 **4** **4**   (icons)

Fresh oregano would work wonderfully in place of dried, especially if you have it growing in your garden or in a windowsill pot. When it's fresh, this herb adds a little sharpness that pairs well with the creamy feta.

4	**(6-inch) whole-wheat pita breads**
1	**tsp olive oil**
1	**zucchini, halved lengthwise and thinly sliced**
¼	**tsp salt**
¼	**tsp black pepper**
1	**large garlic clove, minced**
½	**tsp dried oregano**
16	**cherry tomatoes, halved**
8	**kalamata olives, halved**
¼	**cup crumbled feta**
¼	**cup shredded part-skim mozzarella**
1	**scallion, thinly sliced**

1 Preheat broiler.

2 Place pitas on a large baking sheet. Broil 5 inches from heat until lightly browned, 30 to 60 seconds on each side. Maintain broiler temperature.

3 In a large nonstick skillet over medium heat, warm oil. Add zucchini, salt, and pepper and cook, stirring frequently, until zucchini is tender, about 2 minutes. Add garlic and oregano and cook, stirring constantly until fragrant, 30 seconds.

4 Arrange zucchini mixture evenly on pitas. Top with cherry tomatoes and olives, then sprinkle with feta and mozzarella.

5 Broil 5 inches from heat until cheeses are melted, about 1 minute. Sprinkle with scallion, then cut each pita into 4 wedges.

Per serving (1 pita pizza): 159 Cal, 6 g Total Fat, 2 g Sat Fat, 478 mg Sod, 22 g Total Carb, 4 g Sugar, 3 g Fib, 7 g Prot.

Curry grilled-chicken sandwich with mango salsa

Prep 15 min   Cook 8 min   Serves 1

(6) (4) (4)   ⊛

Indian spices are a great match for grilled chicken, and mango salsa adds cool sweetness. If you can't find mini naan, use pita instead.

Nonstick spray

¼   **cup diced peeled and pitted mango**

2   **tbsp diced cucumber**

1   **tsp minced red onion**

2   **tsp chopped cilantro, plus a few leaves for garnish**

1   **tsp lime juice**

2   **pinches salt**

1   **(1.8-oz) mini naan bread**

½   **tsp Madras curry powder**

1   **(4-oz) boneless skinless chicken breast**

1   In a small cup, combine mango, cucumber, onion, cilantro, lime juice, and 1 pinch salt; set aside. Sprinkle one side of naan with ¼ tsp curry powder. Sprinkle chicken with remaining ¼ tsp curry powder and remaining pinch salt.

2   Coat the rack of outside grill or a grill pan with nonstick spray; heat grill to medium-high heat, or place grill pan over medium-high heat on stovetop. Grill chicken, turning once, until cooked through, about 7 minutes. Grill naan, turning once, until grill marks appear and bread softens, 1 minute.

3   Place chicken on curried side of naan; top with mango salsa and a few leaves of cilantro. Fold and eat.

Per serving (1 sandwich): 300 Cal, 7 g Total Fat, 1 g Sat Fat, 782 mg Sod, 29 g Total Carb, 7 g Sugar, 2 g Fib, 30 g Prot.

Beef and portobello burgers

Prep 15 min Cook 10 min Serves 4

8 8 8

Add minced mushrooms to the ground beef, and two good things happen: Your burgers will be nice and juicy, and they will have an added layer of nutrients.

6	oz portobello mushroom caps
¾	lb (93% lean) ground beef
2	tbsp whole-wheat breadcrumbs
½	tsp salt
¼	tsp black pepper
1	tsp canola oil
¼	cup reduced-fat mayonnaise
2	tbsp chopped basil
1	garlic clove, minced
4	light hamburger rolls or buns, split and toasted
4	thick tomato slices
4	large green leaf lettuce leaves

1 Place mushrooms in a food processor and pulse until minced. Transfer to a large bowl. Add beef, breadcrumbs, salt, and pepper and stir to combine. With damp hands, shape mixture into 4 (½-inch-thick) patties.

2 In a large skillet over medium-high heat, warm oil. Add patties and cook, turning once, until an instant-read thermometer inserted into side of burgers registers 160°F, about 10 minutes. Meanwhile, in a small bowl, stir together mayonnaise, basil, and garlic.

3 Spread mayonnaise mixture evenly on tops of buns. Serve burgers, topped evenly with tomato slices and lettuce leaves, in buns.

Per serving (1 garnished burger): 299 Cal, 13 g Total Fat, 3 g Sat Fat, 640 mg Sod, 24 g Total Carb, 5 g Sugar, 4 g Fib, 23 g Prot.

BBQ pork sandwich with homemade slaw

Prep 10 min   Cook 25 min   Serves 4

(8) (8) (8)   (⌀) (⊘)

Double the recipe and have sandwiches for lunch the next day. Dill pickle slices are a great add-on to serve on the side.

Nonstick spray

1	**lb lean pork tenderloin**
3	**tbsp plus 1 tsp barbecue sauce, divided**
3	**tbsp reduced-fat mayonnaise**
1	**tsp apple-cider vinegar**
⅛	**tsp black pepper**
2	**cups shredded purple cabbage**
3	**tbsp sliced scallion**
4	**mixed-grain hamburger rolls**

1 Preheat oven to 450°F. Line a shallow roasting pan with nonstick foil or spray pan with nonstick spray. (You can also cook the pork on outdoor grill.)

2 Place pork in pan and brush with 2 tbsp barbecue sauce. Roast until an instant read thermometer inserted in center of pork registers 145°F, about 20 minutes. Transfer pork to a cutting board; cover loosely with foil and let stand 10 minutes.

3 Meanwhile, in a medium bowl, whisk mayonnaise, 1 tbsp water, vinegar, and pepper until smooth. Add cabbage and scallion; toss to coat.

4 Cut pork into 20 thin slices. Divide pork evenly among bottoms of rolls; drizzle each with 1 tsp barbecue sauce. Top evenly with slaw and cover with tops of rolls.

Per serving (1 sandwich): 313 Cal, 9 g Total Fat, 2 g Sat Fat, 497 mg Sod, 29 g Total Carb, 9 g Sugar, 3 g Fib, 29 g Prot.

Hawaiian pineapple bowls

Prep 22 min Cook 15 min Serves 4

(4) (3) (3)   (⊘) (⊗)

Want a fun way to liven up a weeknight dinner? Serve it in a pineapple bowl! These are filled with a low-carb fried cauliflower rice that's loaded with shrimp and Canadian bacon.

2	pineapples, about 3 lb each
2	tbsp dark sesame oil, divided
1	lb medium peeled and deveined shrimp
4	oz Canadian bacon, diced
1	medium red bell pepper, diced
1	tbsp minced peeled ginger
¼	tsp crushed red pepper flakes
3	garlic cloves, minced
6	cups cauliflower rice (24 oz)
1	cup sliced scallions
2	tbsp low-sodium soy sauce

1 Cut each pineapple in half lengthwise. Using a paring knife, cut out the core from each half by cutting lengthwise down either side of core, angling knife inward. Discard core. Cut pineapple around the perimeter, leaving a ½-inch shell. Scoop out pineapple flesh with a spoon. Finely chop 1 cup pineapple and set aside. Reserve remaining pineapple for another use.

2 In a large nonstick skillet over medium-high heat, warm 1 tbsp oil. Add shrimp and bacon to pan. Cook until shrimp are just opaque in center and bacon is lightly browned, about 5 minutes; transfer to plate.

3 Add remaining 1 tbsp oil to pan. Add bell pepper, ginger, red pepper flakes, and garlic. Cook, stirring often, until bell pepper is crisp-tender, about 2 minutes. Add cauliflower rice and scallions. Cook, stirring frequently, until cauliflower rice is crisp-tender, about 5 minutes. Stir in shrimp mixture, soy sauce, and chopped pineapple. Cook until heated through, about 1 minute. Divide mixture evenly among pineapple halves.

Per serving (about 2 cups): 365 Cal, 10 g Total Fat, 2 g Sat Fat, 1,232 mg Sod, 46 g Total Carb, 29 g Sugar, 7 g Fib, 29 g Prot.

Perfectly barbecued chicken breasts

Prep 10 min, plus cooling and chilling   Cook 30 min   Serves 8

3 **2** **2**   (grain) (fat) (sugar)

Use either boneless or bone-in chicken for this recipe. Though both will be delicious, cooking chicken on the bone adds even more flavor. A salt brine keeps the meat juicy and moist.

Nonstick spray

½   **cup kosher salt**

4   **(10-oz) skinless, bone-in chicken breasts, halved crosswise**

½   **cup barbecue sauce**

1 In a very large bowl, combine 8 cups warm water and salt and whisk until salt dissolves. Let stand to cool to room temperature, about 30 minutes.

2 Add chicken to brine; cover and refrigerate 1 hour.

3 Spray grill rack with nonstick spray. Prepare gas grill for medium-high, indirect cooking, or build a medium-high-heat charcoal bed in a charcoal grill and rake the coals to the sides of the cooking grate.

4 Remove chicken from brine; rinse and pat dry with paper towels. Place chicken bone-side down on grill rack to the side of heat source, not directly over the heat. Cover and grill 15 minutes.

5 Brush chicken with barbecue sauce, cover and continue cooking until an instant-read thermometer inserted into thickest part of chicken registers 165°F, about 15 minutes (boneless breasts will take less time).

6 Transfer chicken to cutting board, cover loosely with foil, and let stand 5 minutes.

Per serving (3 oz cooked chicken): 166 Cal, 3 g Total Fat, 1 g Sat Fat, 6,019 mg Sod, 7 g Total Carb, 6 g Sugar, 0 g Fib, 26 g Prot.

Slow cooker chicken with chile and corn

Prep 25 min   Cook 7 hr   Serves 4

7 **5** **5**   ⊘ ⊘

Give this stew a sweet heat that stands up to slow cooking by using fresh sweet corn on the cob and fiery serrano chiles.

Nonstick spray

1½   **leeks, white parts only, chopped (about 1 cup)**

1   **cup sliced white mushrooms**

¼   **tsp paprika**

6   **skinless boneless chicken thighs, halved crosswise**

2   **tbsp all-purpose flour**

¼   **tsp salt**

¼   **tsp black pepper**

2   **ears corn, kernels removed**

1   **serrano or jalapeño pepper, seeded and finely chopped**

1   **cup chicken broth**

1 Spray a large skillet with nonstick spray and set over high heat. Add leeks and mushrooms and cook, stirring often, until vegetables are tender, about 3 minutes; transfer to a 5- or 6-qt slow cooker. Wipe out skillet.

2 Place chicken in a large resealable plastic bag. Add flour, paprika, salt, and pepper and shake well to coat chicken.

3 Spray same skillet with nonstick spray and set over medium-high heat. Add chicken and cook, turning occasionally, until browned, 4 to 6 minutes; transfer to slow cooker. Pour chicken broth into skillet, raise heat to high and scrape up any brown bits with a wooden spoon. Pour broth into slow cooker.

4 Add any flour remaining in plastic bag to slow cooker. Top chicken with corn and pepper. (Note: For even more corn flavor, run the dull side of a knife over the corn cob to extract the "milk" into the slow cooker.)

5 Cover and cook until chicken fork-tender and liquid is slightly thickened, 6 to 7 hours on Low.

Per serving (about 1½ cups): 362 Cal, 10 g Total Fat, 3 g Sat Fat, 578 mg Sod, 20 g Total Carb, 4 g Sugar, 2 g Fib, 47 g Prot.

Grilled chicken with mint chimichurri

Prep 10 min Cook 10 min Serves 4

3 1 1   (symbols)

Try this bright, herbaceous sauce on steak or fish. It's fantastic as is, or you can swap in different herbs, like cilantro or tarragon, for more custom combinations.

Nonstick spray

1   cup packed mint leaves
⅔   cup flat-leaf parsley
3   tbsp white-wine vinegar
1   tbsp olive oil
2   garlic cloves, chopped
¾   tsp salt, divided
⅛   tsp red pepper flakes
4   (5-oz) skinless boneless chicken breasts
½   tsp ground cumin
¼   tsp black pepper

1 Spray grill rack with nonstick spray. Preheat grill to medium-high or prepare medium-high fire.

2 Meanwhile, to make chimichurri: In a mini food processor, combine mint, parsley, vinegar, oil, 1 tbsp water, garlic, ¼ tsp salt, and red pepper flakes; puree.

3 Sprinkle chicken with remaining ½ tsp salt, cumin, and black pepper. Place chicken on grill rack and grill, turning once, until chicken is cooked through, 8 to 10 minutes. Serve with chimichurri.

Per serving (1 chicken breast and scant 2 tbsp sauce): 213 Cal, 7 g Total Fat, 1 g Sat Fat, 509 mg Sod, 3 g Total Carb, 0 g Sugar, 2 g Fib, 32 g Prot.

Chili-rubbed pork chops

Prep 10 min, plus chilling Cook 8 min Serves 4

(5) (5) (5)   (꜠) (꜡) (Ꜣ)

Spice rubs are the secret to good barbecue. Although you can use fresh herbs, dried ones make better rubs because they don't burn as quickly over high heat.

Nonstick spray

2   tsp chili powder

1½ tsp packed light brown sugar

1   tsp ground cumin

½   tsp cinnamon

¼   tsp salt

¼   tsp black pepper

4   (5-oz) lean boneless center-cut pork chops, trimmed

4   thyme sprigs

1 In a small bowl, combine chili powder, brown sugar, cumin, cinnamon, salt, and pepper.

2 Place a pork chop on a cutting board. Holding a sharp knife parallel to board and cutting from 1 long side, cut chop ¾ of the way through and open up like a book. Repeat with remaining chops. Rub spice mixture over chops. Place on a plate; cover and refrigerate at least 1 hour or up to 24 hours.

3 Spray a cast iron pan with nonstick spray and set over medium-high heat.

4 Place chops in pan and cook, turning, until an instant-read thermometer inserted into center of each chop registers 145°F, about 4 minutes on each side. Garnish with thyme.

5 Transfer to a platter, cover loosely with foil, and let stand 3 minutes before serving.

Per serving (1 chop): 227 Cal, 9 g Total Fat, 3 g Sat Fat, 249 mg Sod, 3 g Total Carb, 2 g Sugar, 1 g Fib, 31 g Prot.

Flank steak with tomatoes and basil

Prep 5 min, plus chilling   Cook 15 min   Serves 4

5 5 5

Don't use your best aged balsamic for this recipe. The grocery-store variety works fine in this marinade and helps the outside of the steak caramelize as it sears.

1	**lb lean flank steak, trimmed**
¼	**cup plus 1 tbsp balsamic vinegar, divided**
¾	**tsp salt, divided**
¼	**tsp black pepper**
3	**tsp olive oil, divided**
2	**garlic cloves, minced**
3	**cups cherry tomatoes, halved**
⅓	**cup chopped basil**

1 In a large shallow dish, drizzle steak with ¼ cup vinegar and turn to coat. Cover and refrigerate 30 minutes.

2 Remove steak from vinegar and pat dry with paper towels; discard vinegar. Sprinkle steak with ½ tsp salt and pepper.

3 In a large heavy skillet over medium-high heat, warm 2 tsp oil. Add steak and cook, turning occasionally, until an instant-read thermometer inserted into side of steak registers 145°F, 8 to 10 minutes. Transfer to a cutting board and let stand 5 minutes.

4 Meanwhile, in a medium nonstick skillet over medium heat, warm remaining 1 tsp oil. Add garlic and cook, stirring constantly, until fragrant, 30 seconds. Add tomatoes and cook, stirring often, until tomatoes begin to just shrivel, about 4 minutes. Remove from heat and stir in remaining 1 tbsp vinegar, basil, and remaining ¼ tsp salt. Cut steak against grain into 12 thin slices. Serve steak with tomatoes.

Per serving (3 slices steak and about ⅔ cup tomatoes): 231 Cal, 10 g Total Fat, 3 g Sat Fat, 511 mg Sod, 8 g Total Carb, 6 g Sugar, 2 g Fib, 26 g Prot.

Greek yogurt fudge pops

Prep 10 min   Freeze 6 hr   Serves 6

④ ④ ④   🫙 🌾 🍴

Take these chocolaty pops in different flavor directions by adding a few drops of mint extract or a little orange zest when you mix up a batch in the blender.

1	**cup plain fat-free Greek yogurt**
¾	**cup low-fat milk**
6	**tbsp unsweetened cocoa powder**
4½	**tbsp agave nectar**

1 Puree all ingredients in a blender or food processor.

2 Spoon evenly into 6 (⅓-cup) ice pop molds; cover molds with tops. Freeze until completely frozen, at least 6 hours.

Per serving (1 pop): 92 Cal, 1 g Total Fat, 1 g Sat Fat, 27 mg Sod, 18 g Total Carb, 14 g Sugar, 3 g Fib, 6 g Prot.

Blueberry-peach cornmeal cupcakes

Prep 15 min   Cook 20 min   Serves 12

(6) (6) (6)   ⚡ ⊘

Somewhere between a corn muffin and a cupcake, these little treats also turn out beautifully if you use nectarines or plums in place of the peaches.

Nonstick spray

1	**cup all-purpose flour**
1	**cup yellow cornmeal**
2	**tsp baking powder**
½	**tsp baking soda**
½	**tsp salt**
1¼	**cups reduced-fat buttermilk**
½	**cup sugar**
2	**large eggs**
2	**tbsp olive oil**
2	**tsp vanilla extract**
1	**tsp grated lemon zest**
1	**ripe peach, peeled, pitted, and diced (about 1 cup)**
1	**cup fresh or frozen blueberries**
1	**tbsp confectioners' sugar**

1 Preheat oven to 350°F. Spray a 12-cup muffin pan with nonstick spray.

2 In a medium bowl, whisk together flour, cornmeal, baking powder, baking soda, and salt. In a large bowl, whisk together buttermilk, sugar, eggs, oil, vanilla, and lemon zest. Add flour mixture to buttermilk mixture and stir until flour mixture is just moistened. Gently stir in peach and blueberries.

3 Fill muffin cups evenly with batter. Bake until toothpick inserted into centers comes out clean, 18 to 20 minutes. Let cool in pan on a wire rack 5 minutes. Remove cupcakes from pan and cool completely on rack. Just before serving, dust with confectioners' sugar.

Per serving (1 cupcake): 177 Cal, 4 g Total Fat, 1 g Sat Fat, 270 mg Sod, 31 g Total Carb, 13 g Sugar, 1 g Fib, 4 g Prot.

Almond-cherry oat bars

Prep 15 min   Cook 25 min   Serves 16

(5) (5) (4)   (symbol) (symbol)

Make these bars with any favorite berries instead of the cherries if you're looking to mix things up with your summer fruits!

1	**cup white whole-wheat flour**
⅔	**cup old-fashioned rolled oats**
½	**cup sliced almonds, toasted and chopped**
½	**tsp cinnamon**
½	**tsp baking powder**
¼	**tsp baking soda**
¼	**tsp salt**
½	**cup packed dark brown sugar**
¼	**cup olive oil**
2	**large egg whites**
2	**tbsp almond butter**
½	**tsp vanilla extract**
¾	**cup fresh cherries, pitted and halved or unsweetened frozen pitted cherries, halved**

1 Preheat oven to 350°F. Line an 8-inch square baking pan with parchment paper, allowing paper to extend over rim of pan by 2 inches.

2 In a large bowl, stir together flour, oats, almonds, cinnamon, baking powder, baking soda, and salt. In a medium bowl, stir together brown sugar, oil, egg whites, almond butter, and vanilla. Add brown sugar mixture and cherries to flour mixture and stir to combine. Transfer mixture to prepared pan and pat evenly with damp hands.

3 Bake until golden brown and a toothpick inserted into center comes out clean, about 25 minutes.

4 Let cool completely in pan on a wire rack. Lift from pan using parchment paper as handles. Cut lengthwise into 4 strips, then cut each strip crosswise into 4 squares.

Per serving (1 bar): 132 Cal, 6 g Total Fat, 1 g Sat Fat, 80 mg Sod, 16 g Total Carb, 9 g Sugar, 1 g Fib, 3 g Prot.

Fall

Buttermilk-oat pancakes with yogurt and pear

Prep 22 min   Cook 15 min   Serves 4

(9) (8) (6)   (🥕) (❌)

Soaking the oats for a short time makes them soft, creamy, and ready for the pancake batter.

2   **cups fat-free buttermilk**
1   **cup quick-cooking oats**
1   **tbsp honey**
1   **tsp vanilla extract**
1   **large egg, lightly beaten**
¾   **cup white whole-wheat flour**
1   **tsp baking powder**
¼   **tsp baking soda**
½   **tsp ground cinnamon**
¼   **tsp kosher salt**
½   **cup fat-free vanilla Greek yogurt**
1   **large firm-ripe red pear, cored and thinly sliced**

1 In a large bowl, combine buttermilk, oats, honey, and vanilla; let stand 10 minutes.

2 Preheat a large nonstick griddle over medium heat.

3 Stir egg into oat mixture until well combined.

4 In another bowl, combine flour, baking powder, baking soda, cinnamon, and salt; stir flour mixture into oat mixture until just combined.

5 Working in batches, pour batter by ¼-cup measures onto griddle. Cook until bubbles cover pancake tops and edges are browned, 4 to 5 minutes; flip and cook 2 to 3 minutes more. Serve topped with yogurt and pear.

Per serving (3 pancakes, 2 tbsp yogurt, few slices pear): 249 Cal, 3 g Total Fat, 1 g Sat Fat, 457 mg Sod, 52 g Total Carb, 21 g Sugar, 4 g Fib, 14 g Prot.

Breakfast stuffed peppers

Prep 10 min   Cook 20 min   Serves 4

(6) (4) (4)   (⊘) (⊗)

Stuffed peppers get an early-morning makeover with bacon, eggs, and cheese. If you have other fresh herbs handy besides parsley, sprinkle some on.

4   **red bell peppers, tops cut off, seeded**

1   **cup WW Reduced Fat Mexican Blend Shredded Cheese**

4   **slices crisp-cooked bacon, chopped**

4   **large eggs**

Pinch kosher salt (or to taste)

Pinch black pepper (or to taste)

Pinch smoked paprika (or to taste)

Parsley, for garnish

1 Preheat oven to 400°F.

2 In a small baking dish or casserole dish just large enough to hold peppers, stand peppers (if they don't sit upright, cut a thin slice off bottom of each). Evenly divide cheese and bacon among peppers; crack an egg into each. Sprinkle with salt, pepper, and paprika.

3 Bake until egg whites are firm and yolks are slightly runny, 20 to 25 minutes. Garnish with parsley

Per serving (1 stuffed pepper): 219 Cal, 13 g Total Fat, 5 g Sat Fat, 471 mg Sod, 9 g Total Carb, 5 g Sugar, 2 g Fib, 17 g Prot.

Irish oatmeal with roasted apples

Prep 12 min   Cook 30 min   Serves 4

(7) (7) (2)   (symbols)

Give yourself a treat in the morning with this oatmeal made with steel-cut oats. Its toothsome texture and sweet spiciness make it breakfast perfection.

2	**Honeycrisp or Rome apples, cored and cut into 1-inch chunks**
1	**tbsp packed brown sugar**
½	**tsp ground cinnamon**
⅛	**tsp salt**
1	**cup steel-cut oats**
2	**tbsp seedless golden raisins**
2	**tbsp chopped toasted walnuts**

1 Preheat oven to 375°F. Line a rimmed baking sheet with parchment paper.

2 In a medium bowl, combine apples, brown sugar, and cinnamon and toss to coat. Place apples on prepared baking sheet and spread out to form a single layer. Bake, stirring once, until apples are tender, about 30 minutes.

3 Meanwhile, in a large saucepan, bring 3 cups water and salt to a boil. Stir in oats and raisins. Reduce heat and simmer, stirring often, until liquid is absorbed and oatmeal is tender but still chewy, about 30 minutes.

4 Divide oatmeal among 4 bowls and top with apples and walnuts.

Per serving (⅔ cup oatmeal, about ½ cup apples, and ½ tbsp walnuts): 249 Cal, 5 g Total Fat, 0 g Sat Fat, 81 mg Sod, 47 g Total Carb, 17 g Sugar, 7 g Fib, 6 g Prot.

Pumpkin-pie butter

Prep 6 min   No cook   Serves 12

① ① ①   ⊙ ✅ ⊘ ⊘

Enjoy your favorite autumn flavors any time of year with this luscious spread. Serve as a dip with apple or pear slices, pretzel sticks, or biscotti; slather it over toast, waffles, or pizzelles; or swirl it into oatmeal or Greek yogurt.

1	**(15-oz) can pumpkin puree**
½	**cup unsweetened powdered almond butter**
2	**tbsp maple syrup**
2	**tsp pumpkin pie spice**
1	**tsp vanilla extract**
¾	**tsp apple-cider vinegar**
¼	**tsp salt**

1 In a large bowl, combine all ingredients. Whisk until well blended.

Per serving (2½ tbsp): 38 Cal, 1 g Total Fat, 0 g Sat Fat, 51 mg Sod, 6 g Total Carb, 4 g Sugar, 2 g Fib, 2 g Prot.

Chopped spinach and pear salad

Prep 15 min   No cook   Serves 4

Pomegranate seeds lend gorgeous color and a burst of tartness to salads. Cut back on prep time by buying them pre-packaged.

4	**cups lightly packed baby spinach (about 5 oz), chopped**
1	**cup chopped endive**
1	**firm-ripe pear, preferably d'Anjou, cored and chopped**
⅓	**cup pomegranate seeds**
1	**tbsp minced shallot**
1	**tbsp sherry vinegar**
1	**tbsp extra-virgin olive oil**
½	**tsp Dijon mustard**
½	**tsp honey**
¼	**tsp salt**
⅛	**tsp black pepper**

1 In a large bowl, combine spinach, endive, pear, and pomegranate seeds.

2 In a cruet or small jar with a tightly fitting lid, combine shallot, vinegar, oil, 1 tbsp water, mustard, honey, salt, and pepper; shake well.

3 Pour dressing over salad and toss to coat.

Per serving (about 1½ cups): 80 Cal, 4 g Total Fat, 1 g Sat Fat, 188 mg Sod, 12 g Total Carb, 7 g Sugar, 3 g Fib, 1 g Prot.

Apple-cider chicken salad

Prep 15 min   Cook 20 min, plus chilling   Serves 4

6 5 5

Sweet and savory ingredients like apples, pecans, blue cheese, and Dijon mustard join forces to transform everyday chicken salad into a memorable meal.

4	**tbsp apple-cider vinegar, divided**
2	**tbsp chopped chives, divided**
1	**tbsp plus 1 tsp Dijon mustard, divided**
1	**tsp kosher salt, divided**
½	**tsp black pepper, divided**
1	**lb boneless skinless chicken breast**
1	**tbsp extra-virgin olive oil**
10	**cups mixed salad greens**
1	**large red apple, cored and thinly sliced**
⅓	**cup toasted pecans, chopped**
¼	**cup crumbled blue cheese**

1 In a wide shallow bowl, whisk together 2 tbsp vinegar, 1 tbsp chives, 1 tbsp mustard, ½ tsp salt, and ¼ tsp pepper; add chicken and turn to coat. Cover chicken and marinate in refrigerator, turning chicken once or twice, about 30 minutes.

2 Preheat oven to 350°F.

3 Remove chicken from marinade and place in a baking dish; discard marinade. Cover chicken with foil; bake until chicken is just cooked through and reaches an internal temperature of 165°F, 20 to 25 minutes. Let chicken cool slightly, then transfer to a cutting board; cut diagonally into thick slices.

4 Meanwhile, in a cup or small bowl, whisk together oil, remaining 2 tbsp vinegar, remaining 1 tsp mustard, remaining ½ tsp salt, and remaining ¼ tsp pepper; set aside.

5 When ready to serve: In a large serving bowl, combine greens, apple, pecans, and blue cheese; drizzle with 2 tbsp vinaigrette and toss to coat. Place chicken over salad. Stir any juices from baking dish into remaining vinaigrette and drizzle over chicken; garnish with remaining 1 tbsp chives.

Per serving (about 2½ cups salad and 3 oz cooked chicken): 325 Cal, 15 g Total Fat, 3 g Sat Fat, 776 mg Sod, 15 g Total Carb, 6 g Sugar, 5 g Fib, 31 g Prot.

Grilled cheddar-cheese sandwiches

Prep 10 min   Cook 6 min   Serves 4

⑥ ⑥ ⑥   (🥕) (🚫)

Use this savory cream cheese spread to elevate your basic grilled cheese.

Nonstick spray

¼ **cup low-fat cream cheese (Neufchâtel)**

3 **tbsp minced shallot**

4 **tsp whole-grain mustard**

1 **tbsp minced unsweetened dill pickles or bread-and-butter pickles**

8 **slices reduced-calorie bread**

¾ **cup WW Reduced Fat Mexican Blend Shredded Cheese**

1 In a small bowl, combine cream cheese, shallot, mustard, and pickles; spread about 1 tbsp cream cheese mixture on one side of each piece of bread. Top 4 slices of bread with 3 tbsp shredded cheese each; cover with remaining bread slices, cream cheese-side down.

2 Coat a large skillet with nonstick spray. Place over medium heat and add sandwiches; cook, flipping sandwiches once, until bread is toasted and cheese melts, 2 to 3 minutes per side.

Per serving (1 sandwich): 180 Cal, 7 g Total Fat, 4 g Sat Fat, 467 mg Sod, 24 g Total Carb, 4 g Sugar, 5 g Fib, 10 g Prot.

Butternut squash–crust fontina pizza

Prep 20 min   Cook 45 min   Serves 4

(6) (5) (5)   (☺) (⊗)

Mashed butternut squash forms the base of this pizza crust. Besides being a great way to eat more veggies, it adds sweetness to the pie.

Nonstick spray

1½ **cups cooked cubed butternut squash, mashed**

½   **cup all-purpose flour**

½   **cup plus ⅓ cup shredded part-skim mozzarella, divided**

1   **tbsp grated Parmesan**

1   **large egg, beaten**

2½ **tsp minced sage, divided**

½   **tsp baking powder**

½   **tsp kosher salt**

¼   **tsp granulated garlic**

2   **pinches ground nutmeg, divided**

Pinch cayenne pepper

⅓   **cup shredded fontina**

1 Preheat oven to 375°F. Line a large rimmed baking sheet with parchment paper; coat with nonstick spray.

2 In a large bowl, combine mashed squash, flour, ½ cup mozzarella, Parmesan, egg, ½ tsp sage, baking powder, salt, garlic, 1 pinch nutmeg, and cayenne; mix well. Spoon crust mixture into two 8-inch circles on prepared pan; smooth with a spoon to form an even layer. Bake until crusts are browned on bottom, about 25 minutes. Carefully flip crusts and bake until evenly browned, about 15 minutes more.

3 In a medium bowl, combine fontina and remaining ⅓ cup mozzarella; scatter evenly across cooked crusts and sprinkle with remaining 2 tsp sage. Return pizzas to oven; bake until cheese melts, 5 to 7 minutes. Garnish with remaining pinch nutmeg; cut each pizza into 4 slices and serve.

Per serving (2 slices): 219 Cal, 9 g Total Fat, 5 g Sat Fat, 585 mg Sod, 18 g Total Carb, 1 g Sugar, 3 g Fib, 13 g Prot.

Butternut squash noodles with turkey

Prep 15 min   Cook 8 min   Serves 1

5 **4** **4**

Spiralize your own squash noodles or look for them already prepped in the produce section of your supermarket.

Nonstick spray

1¼ tsp unsalted butter, divided

4   oz (about 1½ cups) spiralized butternut squash noodles

½   Gala or Granny Smith apple, cored and cut into chunks

1   large shallot, sliced

½   cup diced cooked skinless turkey breast

¼   cup fat-free chicken broth

1½ tsp chopped thyme

Pinch salt

Pinch black pepper

½   tsp grated lemon zest

1½ tbsp toasted chopped walnuts

1 Coat a medium skillet with nonstick spray; add ½ tsp butter and melt over medium heat.

2 Add squash noodles, apple, and shallot; raise heat to medium-high, cover skillet, and cook, stirring occasionally, until noodles begin to soften, about 3 minutes.

3 Stir in turkey, broth, thyme, salt, and pepper; cook, uncovered, stirring occasionally, until noodles are tender, about 3 minutes.

4 Stir in remaining ¾ tsp butter and lemon zest; moisten with additional broth, if desired. Transfer to a bowl or plate, sprinkle with walnuts, and serve.

Per serving (1 bowl): 346 Cal, 14 g Total Fat, 4 g Sat Fat, 571 mg Sod, 37 g Total Carb, 16 g Sugar, 7 g Fib, 22 g Prot.

Pasta with creamy butternut squash and sage

Prep 10 min   Cook 2 min   Serves 1

8 8 8   🥄 🚫

Here's a great go-to lunch or dinner when you've got leftover pasta. Microwaving the dish gets dinner on the table in a flash, but if you have more time, you can stir the ingredients together in a skillet over medium heat until the cheese melts and the pasta is very hot.

1	**cup cooked rigatoni**
½	**cup cooked cubed butternut squash**
1½	**tbsp low-fat cream cheese (Neufchâtel), softened**
1	**tbsp chopped sage**
1½	**tbsp grated Pecorino Romano**

Pinch salt (or to taste)

Pinch black pepper (or to taste)

1 In a microwavable bowl, toss together rigatoni, squash, cream cheese, 1 tbsp water, and sage. Cover and microwave until hot, about 2 minutes. Sprinkle with Pecorino Romano; stir and season with salt and pepper.

Per serving (1 bowl): 331 Cal, 8 g Total Fat, 4 g Sat Fat, 517 mg Sod, 47 g Total Carb, 1 g Sugar, 6 g Fib, 11 g Prot.

Orecchiette with roasted Brussels sprouts and grapes

Prep 20 min   Cook 40 min   Serves 4

6 6 6

Roasted fruit and veggies make up most of this dish, so it's light on pasta but full of great flavors.

1   **lb Brussels sprouts, halved if small or quartered if large**

2   **cups seedless red grapes**

1   **large onion, chopped**

2   **garlic cloves, minced**

1   **tbsp thyme leaves**

2   **tsp olive oil**

1   **tsp salt**

1   **tsp black pepper**

1   **cup orecchiette**

4   **tbsp crumbled goat cheese**

4   **tsp balsamic vinegar**

1 Preheat oven to 400°F.

2 On a large rimmed baking sheet, combine Brussels sprouts, grapes, onion, garlic, thyme, oil, salt, and pepper. Toss and spread out evenly. Roast until Brussels sprouts are tender and grapes are juicy, stirring once or twice, 35 to 40 minutes.

3 Meanwhile, cook pasta according to package directions. Drain pasta and return it to the pot. Add roasted Brussels sprouts mixture, including juices; stir well. Divide among 4 bowls; garnish each with 1 tbsp goat cheese and 1 tsp vinegar.

Per serving (1½ cups): 290 Cal, 6 g Total Fat, 3 g Sat Fat, 685 mg Sod, 50 g Total Carb, 17 g Sugar, 7 g Fib, 11 g Prot.

Cooking tip
Cut all the Brussels sprouts a similar size so they roast evenly.

Tofu, broccoli, and squash with tahini

Prep 25 min   Cook 40 min   Serves 4

(5) (3) (3)   (🥕) (✂)

Serve this yummy protein-and-veggie creation as a vegetarian main, or try it as a side dish. The creamy tahini-yogurt sauce has a nice kick, thanks to a little sriracha.

1	(14-oz) package extra-firm tofu, drained, blotted dry, and cut into 8 equal pieces
1	tbsp low-sodium soy sauce
1	large head broccoli, cut into florets
4	tsp extra-virgin olive oil, divided
1¼	tsp kosher salt (or to taste), divided
½	tsp black pepper (or to taste), divided
2	lb butternut squash, peeled, seeded, and cut into 1½-in chunks
2	garlic cloves, thinly sliced
2	tbsp tahini
2	tbsp plain fat-free Greek yogurt
2	tbsp lemon juice
2	tbsp warm water
1	tsp sriracha, or to taste
2	tbsp green pumpkin seeds (pepitas), toasted

1 Preheat oven to 450°F.

2 Place tofu in a bowl, sprinkle with soy sauce, and let sit for 10 minutes.

3 In a medium bowl, toss broccoli with 2 tsp oil, ½ tsp salt, and ¼ tsp pepper.

4 On a large sheet pan, toss squash with remaining 2 tsp oil, ½ tsp salt, remaining ¼ tsp pepper, and garlic; roast 15 minutes. Remove pan from oven and stir; move squash to one side of pan.

5 Spread broccoli out on other side of pan; nestle tofu down center of pan, making sure each piece makes contact with pan. Return to oven; cook until squash is tender, 20 to 25 minutes.

6 Meanwhile, in a small bowl, combine tahini, yogurt, lemon juice, water, remaining ¼ tsp salt, and sriracha.

7 Divide tofu and vegetables between 4 plates or place on a platter; drizzle with tahini sauce and sprinkle with pumpkin seeds.

Per serving (2 pieces tofu, 1¼ cups vegetables, 1½ tbsp tahini, and ½ tbsp pumpkin seeds): 359 Cal, 15 g Total Fat, 2 g Sat Fat, 813 mg Sod, 44 g Total Carb, 8 g Sugar, 11 g Fib, 20 g Prot.

Roasted salmon with chickpeas

Prep 25 min   Cook 30 min   Serves 4

(9) (2) (2)   (🌾) (🥜)

Beautiful colors and complex flavors make this sheet-pan dinner a stand out. Leftovers hold up well for several days in the fridge and reheat well.

1½	**tsp smoked paprika**
1	**tsp ground coriander**
1	**tsp ground cumin**
1	**tsp kosher salt**
¾	**tsp black pepper**
2	**zucchini, cut into 1-inch chunks**
1	**red bell pepper, chopped**
1	**medium red onion, thinly sliced**
1	**(15½-oz) can chickpeas, drained, rinsed, and patted dry**
1	**tbsp plus 1 tsp extra-virgin olive oil, divided**
1	**lb skinless wild salmon fillet, cut into 4 equal pieces**
4	**tbsp plain fat-free Greek yogurt**
2	**tbsp mint leaves**
4	**lemon wedges**

1 Preheat oven to 450°F.

2 In a small bowl, stir together paprika, coriander, cumin, salt, and pepper; set aside.

3 On a large baking sheet, combine zucchini, bell pepper, onion, and chickpeas. Sprinkle with 1 tbsp oil and 4 tsp spice mixture. Toss well to coat; spread in a single layer and roast 20 minutes.

4 Meanwhile, coat salmon with remaining 1 tsp oil and remaining spice mixture; set aside. Remove baking sheet from oven; toss vegetables with a spatula. Clear 4 spaces so salmon can sit right on pan; nestle salmon in spaces. Return to oven; roast for another 10 minutes or until salmon is cooked to your liking.

5 Dollop 1 tbsp yogurt over each piece of salmon; garnish salmon and vegetables with mint. Serve with lemon wedges.

Per serving (1 piece salmon, 1 cup vegetable mixture, and 1 tbsp yogurt): 404 Cal, 15 g Total Fat, 2 g Sat Fat, 815 mg Sod, 35 g Total Carb, 10 g Sugar, 10 g Fib, 34 g Prot.

Garlic, rosemary, and lemon oven fries

Prep 15 min   Cook 45 min   Serves 6

These hot, crispy fries have a tasty Italian influence. Make sure to use a rimmed baking sheet so all the fries stay in the pan when you slide it into and take it out of the oven!

Nonstick spray

2	lb (about 5 medium) Yukon gold potatoes
1	tbsp olive oil
1	tbsp minced rosemary leaves
2	tsp minced garlic
1	tsp minced lemon zest
½	tsp salt
½	tsp black pepper

1 Preheat oven to 425°F. Line a large rimmed baking sheet with a silicone baking mat or parchment paper.

2 Cut potatoes into ½-inch-thick slices; cut slices into ½-inch-thick sticks (you should have about 60 fries). Spread fries on prepared baking sheet, making sure they don't overlap or touch; coat with nonstick spray. Bake for 40 minutes, turning fries every 10 minutes.

3 Meanwhile, in a small bowl, combine oil, rosemary, garlic, lemon zest, salt, and pepper. After fries have cooked, remove from oven and sprinkle with oil mixture; toss well. Bake until aromatic and browned, about 5 minutes more. Transfer pan to a wire rack and cool for a few minutes; sprinkle fries with any herb mixture on baking sheet before serving.

Per serving (10 fries): 128 Cal, 3 g Total Fat, 0 g Sat Fat, 218 mg Sod, 24 g Total Carb, 2 g Sugar, 4 g Fib, 3 g Prot.

Serving idea
For a dependable dipping sauce, stir together fat-free Greek yogurt, a little reduced-fat mayonnaise, a squeeze of lemon juice and pinch of zest, salt, pepper, and a dash of garlic powder.

Mashed butternut squash and apples

Prep 10 min Cook 12 min Serves 6

(1) (1) (1)   (symbols)

Special enough for holiday entertaining and easy enough for a busy weeknight, since you cook it in the microwave. Look for already peeled and cubed butternut squash in the produce section of your grocery store; it's an incredible time-saver.

20 oz butternut squash, peeled and cubed

2 medium apples, peeled, cored, and cut into small pieces

½ cup apple cider

1 tbsp butter, cut into pieces

1½ tsp chopped thyme

½ tsp table salt

¼ tsp black pepper

1 In a shallow microwave-safe baking dish or container, place squash, apples, and cider and sprinkle butter on top. Cover and microwave until tender, about 10 to 12 minutes. Mash until smooth, yet slightly chunky; stir in thyme, salt, and pepper.

Per serving (⅔ cup): 97 Cal, 2 g Total Fat, 1 g Sat Fat, 198 mg Sod, 21 g Total Carb, 11 g Sugar, 3 g Fib, 1 g Prot.

Roasted cauliflower with lemon, garlic, and parsley

Prep 10 min   Cook 30 min   Serves 8

Roasting cauliflower brings out its nutty side and natural sweetness. Fresh parsley, lemon zest, and garlic add bright, bold taste.

2	heads cauliflower
1	tbsp olive oil
1	tsp kosher salt
1½	tbsp minced parsley
1½	tsp minced lemon zest
1	tsp minced garlic

1 Preheat oven to 450°F. Line 2 large baking sheets with parchment paper.

2 Cut cauliflower into bite-size pieces; rinse in a colander and pat dry. Place cauliflower in a large bowl and drizzle with oil; sprinkle with salt and toss to coat.

3 Spread florets evenly on prepared pans. Roast, stirring once halfway through, until well-browned, about 30 minutes. Toss cauliflower with parsley, lemon zest, and garlic.

Per serving (⅔ cup): 52 Cal, 2 g Total Fat, 0 g Sat Fat, 285 mg Sod, 8 g Total Carb, 3 g Sugar, 4 g Fib, 3 g Prot.

Chicken piccata stir-fry

Prep 20 min   Cook 5 min   Serves 4

4 2 2

Lemon brightens up this stir-fry, but we suggest adding it after the food is plated. If an acidic ingredient like lemon juice is added to the wok, it may ruin the pan's patina.

1   **lb boneless skinless chicken breast, cut into ¼-inch-thick slices**

3   **tbsp dry sherry, divided**

2   **tsp cornstarch, divided**

¾   **tsp salt, divided**

¼   **tsp black pepper**

½   **cup fat-free chicken broth**

1   **tbsp low-sodium soy sauce**

1   **tbsp plus 1 tsp peanut oil or vegetable oil, divided**

1   **shallot, thinly sliced**

1   **tbsp minced garlic**

2   **cups green beans, cut into 2-inch lengths**

1   **tbsp capers, drained and rinsed**

2   **tbsp chopped parsley**

½   **lemon, cut into 4 wedges**

1 In a medium bowl, combine chicken, 1 tbsp sherry, 1 tsp cornstarch, ½ tsp salt, and pepper. In a small bowl, combine broth, soy sauce, remaining 2 tbsp sherry, and remaining 1 tsp cornstarch.

2 Heat a 14-inch flat-bottomed wok or 12-inch skillet over high heat until a drop of water evaporates within 1 to 2 seconds of contact; swirl in 1 tbsp oil. Add shallot and garlic; stir-fry 10 seconds or until fragrant. Push shallot mixture to sides of wok and add chicken; spread evenly in one layer. Cook undisturbed 1 minute, letting chicken begin to sear. Stir-fry until chicken is no longer pink but not cooked through, about 1 minute.

3 Swirl in remaining 1 tsp oil. Add green beans and capers and sprinkle with remaining ¼ tsp salt; stir-fry 30 seconds or until just combined. Swirl in broth mixture; stir-fry 1 to 2 minutes or until chicken is cooked through and sauce has slightly thickened. Sprinkle on parsley; serve with lemon wedges.

Per serving (1 cup): 231 Cal, 8 g Total Fat, 1 g Sat Fat, 742 mg Sod, 10 g Total Carb, 3 g Sugar, 2 g Fib, 27 g Prot.

Oven-fried paprika chicken cutlets

Prep 14 min   Cook 10 min   Serves 4

(4) (2) (2)   (✣)

Give classic breaded chicken cutlets great crunch and a flavor bump by using saltine crackers and a generous dose of paprika for the coating.

Nonstick spray

½   cup plain fat-free yogurt

3   tsp sweet paprika, divided

15 saltine crackers, crushed into crumbs

1   tsp salt

¼   tsp black pepper

4   (¼-lb) thin-cut boneless skinless chicken cutlets

1   tbsp chopped parsley

4   lemon wedges

1 Preheat broiler and coat a baking sheet with nonstick spray.

2 Place yogurt and 1 tsp paprika in a small shallow bowl; mix to combine. On a large shallow plate, combine cracker crumbs, salt, pepper, and remaining 2 tsp paprika; stir to just blend. Place each chicken cutlet in yogurt mixture and turn to coat. Next, place chicken in crumb mixture, turning to coat both sides and pressing lightly to adhere crumbs.

3 Place coated chicken on prepared baking sheet and lightly spray with nonstick spray. Broil 3 to 4 inches from heat source until golden brown and cooked through, flipping once, 4 to 5 minutes per side.

4 Serve sprinkled with parsley and garnished with lemon wedges.

Per serving (1 piece chicken): 207 Cal, 4 g Total Fat, 1 g Sat Fat, 761 mg Sod, 13 g Total Carb, 3 g Sugar, 1 g Fib, 28 g Prot.

Sesame chicken

Prep 20 min   Cook 10 min   Serves 4

(5) (3) (3)   (Ⓩ)

Most restaurant versions of this dish are deep-fried. But pan-searing keeps all the classic flavor with only a fraction of the fat.

2	**tbsp sesame seeds**
1	**tbsp low-sodium soy sauce**
1	**tbsp maple syrup**
1	**tbsp sherry (dry or sweet)**
1	**tsp minced ginger**
½	**tsp five-spice powder**
2	**tbsp all-purpose flour**
½	**tsp salt**
¼	**tsp black pepper**
1	**lb boneless skinless chicken breast, cut into 2-inch strips**
2	**tsp peanut oil**

1 Place a large nonstick skillet over medium-high heat. Add sesame seeds and cook until lightly toasted, shaking pan frequently, 2 to 3 minutes; transfer seeds to a shallow dish and set aside.

2 In a small bowl, whisk together 1 tbsp water, soy sauce, maple syrup, sherry, ginger, and five-spice powder; set aside.

3 In a shallow dish, combine flour, salt, and pepper; add chicken and turn to coat. Shake chicken pieces to remove excess flour.

4 In a large nonstick skillet over medium-high heat, warm oil. Add chicken and cook, turning pieces occasionally, until browned on all sides, about 5 minutes. Add soy sauce mixture to chicken and cook until sauce thickens and is almost evaporated, 2 to 3 minutes more.

5 Thread cooked chicken onto wooden skewers. Dip in toasted sesame seeds and serve drizzled with any additional soy sauce mixture.

Per serving (about 4 chicken strips): 218 Cal, 7 g Total Fat, 1 g Sat Fat, 471 mg Sod, 8 g Total Carb, 3 g Sugar, 1 g Fib, 27 g Prot.

Pot roast with gravy

Prep 15 min Cook 3 hrs Serves 8

⑥ ⑥ ⑥   ⊘ ⊘ ⊘

Serve this dish with noodles or mashed potatoes to absorb the gravy. Leftovers make incredible sandwiches.

Nonstick spray

1½ tbsp sweet paprika

1   tbsp packed dark brown sugar

1½ tsp salt

1   tsp black pepper

3   lb lean beef brisket, trimmed, patted dry

2½ lb onions, sliced

3   small carrots, sliced

2   bay leaves

1 Preheat oven to 325°F.

2 In a small bowl, combine paprika, sugar, salt, and pepper; rub mixture all over brisket.

3 Coat a large Dutch oven with nonstick spray; place over medium-high heat. Sear brisket until well-browned on outside (including edges), 3 to 5 minutes per side; remove brisket and set aside. Add onions, carrots, bay leaves, and ¼ cup water to pot, scraping the bottom to incorporate any browned bits. Place brisket on top of vegetables and cover pot with lid; place in oven and cook for 2 hours.

4 Remove pot from oven and transfer brisket to a cutting board; cut meat into ¼-inch-thick slices. Keep slices together so the brisket is in the same shape as before you cut it.

5 Working in batches, process vegetable mixture in a blender or food processor until smooth. Pour half of pureed gravy back into pot, carefully place meat on top, and pour remaining gravy over meat. Cover pot and place back in oven; cook for 1 more hour.

Per serving (4 to 5 slices meat and ½ cup gravy): 340 Cal, 13 g Total Fat, 4 g Sat Fat, 589 mg Sod, 19 g Total Carb, 9 g Sugar, 4 g Fib, 37 g Prot.

Cooking tip
You can cook the meat on top of the stove over low heat instead of baking it. Season the gravy with salt just before serving, if desired.

Roasted brisket

Prep 20 min   Cook 3 hrs   Serves 8

(6) (6) (6)   (🚫) (🚫) (🚫)

Toss some potatoes in the oven to serve along with this lightened-up autumn classic, which is also a Jewish holiday tradition.

1	**large onion, sliced**
2	**garlic cloves, minced**
1	**lb baby carrots**
5	**oz mushrooms, sliced (about 2 to 2½ cups)**
2½	**lb lean beef brisket, trimmed**
1	**(28-oz) can crushed tomatoes**
2	**tbsp lemon juice**
2	**tbsp sugar**
1	**tsp paprika**
¾	**tsp salt**
¼	**tsp black pepper**
¼	**tsp red pepper flakes**

1 Preheat oven to 325°F.

2 On bottom of a nonstick roasting pan, spread onion and garlic; top with carrots and mushrooms. Place beef over vegetables.

3 In a medium bowl, combine tomatoes, lemon juice, sugar, paprika, salt, black pepper, and red pepper flakes; stir to dissolve sugar. Pour tomato mixture over brisket and vegetables. Cover the pan tightly with a sheet of heavy-duty aluminum foil. Roast for 2 hours.

4 Remove pan from oven; uncover, stir, and use pan juices to baste brisket. Return pan to oven and roast for about 1 hour more, uncovered, basting every 15 minutes.

5 Remove pan from oven and let stand for 10 minutes before cutting beef across the grain into ¼-inch-thick slices. Serve meat and vegetables with sauce spooned over top.

Per serving (3 oz beef and ¾ cup vegetables with sauce): 283 Cal, 11 g Total Fat, 4 g Sat Fat, 514 mg Sod, 16 g Total Carb, 10 g Sugar, 3 g Fib, 31 g Prot.

Slow cooker winter vegetable and farro stew

Serves 6   Prep 30 min   Cook 4 hr

Feel free to mix up the vegetables here, using any kind of winter squash and mushrooms you like.

6	medium cloves, chopped, divided
½	cup chopped parsley
½	tsp salt (or to taste), divided
¼	tsp black pepper (or to taste), divided, plus a pinch
2	tbsp olive oil
2	tsp fennel seed
1	medium fennel bulb, chopped
1	medium yellow onion, chopped
10	oz mushrooms such as shiitake, cremini, or button, cut into bite-size pieces
2	lb kabocha or butternut squash, peeled, seeded, cut into ½-inch pieces (about 4 cups)
28	oz canned whole San Marzano tomatoes, crushed
4	cups fat-free reduced-sodium vegetable broth
¾	cup farro, rinsed
¾	cup dry lentils, rinsed
1	oz Parmesan, shaved

1 In a small bowl, combine a third of garlic with parsley; season with a pinch each salt and pepper, and set aside.

2 If you have a slow cooker insert that you can saute in on the stovetop, use it to heat oil over medium-high heat. Add fennel seed and remaining garlic; cook, stirring, until fragrant and fennel and garlic begin to smell toasty, about 2 minutes. Add fennel bulb, onion, and mushrooms and season with ¼ tsp salt and ⅛ tsp pepper; cook, stirring occasionally, until vegetables are softened and beginning to brown, about 10 minutes. (Alternatively, you can saute vegetables in a large skillet and transfer to slow cooker at this stage).

3 Add squash, tomatoes, broth, farro, and lentils to slow cooker; season with ¼ tsp salt and ⅛ tsp pepper (or to taste). Cover slow cooker and set heat to High; cook until farro, lentils, and squash are completely cooked through, 4 hours. Uncover, stir and season to taste, if needed. Serve topped with garlic-parsley mixture and Parmesan.

Per serving (2½ cups): 345 Cal, 7 g Total Fat, 2 g Sat Fat, 605 mg Sod, 61 g Total Carb, 10 g Sugar, 11 g Fib, 11 g Prot.

Cooking tip

This can be made stovetop as well; just make sure to use a large heavy-bottomed pot. Cook as instructed (replacing slow cooker with a Dutch oven or soup pot), and reduce the cook time to 1½ hours.

Slow cooker red beans and rice

Prep 20 min   Cook 3½ hrs   Serves 4

(6) (3) (3)   (wheat-free) (dairy-free) (nut-free)

Smoky, spicy chipotle sauce adds robust heat and flavor. For a milder taste, substitute tomato sauce and a dash of chili powder.

Nonstick spray

1	**small onion, chopped**
1	**garlic clove, minced**
½	**cup converted white rice**
1½	**cups fat-free chicken broth**
1	**(14 ½-oz) can tomato puree**
1	**(15-oz) can kidney beans**
2	**slices reduced-fat bacon, cooked until crisp and crumbled**
2	**tbsp canned chipotle sauce**
½	**tsp dried oregano**
½	**tsp salt**
¼	**tsp black pepper**
1	**tbsp chopped cilantro**
1	**tbsp chopped scallion greens**

1 Coat a large skillet with nonstick spray and place over medium-high heat. Add onion and garlic to skillet and cook, stirring, until softened, 2 to 3 minutes.

2 Place rice, broth, tomato puree, beans, bacon, chipotle sauce, oregano, salt, and pepper in a 3- to 4-qt slow cooker; add onion and garlic. Cover and cook on Low for 3½ hours; stir in cilantro and scallion just before serving.

Per serving (about 1 cup): 249 Cal, 2 g Total Fat, 0 g Sat Fat, 1,368 mg Sod, 46 g Total Carb, 8 g Sugar, 8 g Fib, 11 g Prot.

Prep ahead
Start this dish on a weekend morning and you'll have lunch waiting for you. Converted (aka parboiled) rice is sometimes recommended in slow cooker recipes since the grains don't clump together as much as regular white rice grains do. You can, however, use regular rice in this recipe if you'd prefer.

Whole-wheat chili mac

Prep 10 min Cook 30 min Serves 6

5 **4** **2**   🚫 🚫

Top this hearty weeknight dish with a little grated Parmesan, low-fat sour cream, or reduced-fat Mexican-blend shredded cheese. And sprinkle on some chopped cilantro or parsley if you have it on hand.

¾ **lb (93% lean) ground beef**

1 **medium onion, diced**

1 **(14½-oz) can Mexican-style stewed tomatoes with juice**

1¼ **cups canned tomato sauce**

2 **tbsp drained canned green chiles, chopped**

2 **tsp chili powder**

1 **tsp ground cumin**

1 **cup whole-wheat elbow macaroni**

1 **(15-oz) can kidney beans, rinsed and drained**

1 In a large skillet over medium-high heat, combine beef and onion. Cook, breaking up chunks of meat, until meat is browned, about 10 minutes. Tilt skillet to drain off excess fat. Stir in stewed tomatoes and juice, tomato sauce, chiles, chili powder, and cumin; bring to a boil.

2 Stir in macaroni and beans. Return to a boil, reduce heat, cover, and simmer until macaroni is tender, about 15 minutes.

Per serving (about 1¼ cups): 247 Cal, 5 g Total Fat, 2 g Sat Fat, 676 mg Sod, 33 g Total Carb, 6 g Sugar, 7 g Fib, 20 g Prot.

Carrot-apple Bundt cake

Prep 15 min   Cook 45 min, plus cooling   Serves 24

This pretty cake is topped with an irresistible cream-cheese glaze. You have to wait for the cake to cool before drizzling it on, so hang in there!

Nonstick spray

2½ cups all-purpose flour

2½ tsp baking powder

2   tsp cinnamon

½   tsp baking soda

½   tsp salt

1   cup granulated sugar

¾   cup packed brown sugar

3   large eggs

⅓   cup canola oil

1   tbsp plus ⅛ tsp vanilla extract, divided

¾   lb carrots, shredded

1   apple, peeled, cored, and diced

½   cup dried cranberries

1¼ cups confectioners' sugar

2   tbsp reduced-fat cream cheese (Neufchâtel)

1   tbsp plus 1 tsp low-fat (1%) milk

1 Preheat oven 350°F. Spray a 10-inch Bundt pan with nonstick spray.

2 In a medium bowl, whisk together flour, baking powder, cinnamon, baking soda, and salt.

3 In a large bowl, using an electric mixer on medium speed, beat granulated sugar, brown sugar, and eggs until thickened, about 2 minutes. Add oil and 1 tbsp vanilla and beat until blended. With mixer on low speed, beat in flour mixture just until blended (batter will be thick). Add carrots, apple, and cranberries and stir just until blended.

4 Spoon batter into prepared pan and smooth top. Bake until a toothpick inserted into center of cake comes out clean, 40 to 45 minutes. Let cake cool in pan on a wire rack for 10 minutes. Remove cake from pan and let cool completely on rack.

5 To make glaze: In a large bowl, using electric mixer on low speed, beat confectioners' sugar, cream cheese, 1 tbsp of milk, and remaining ⅛ tsp vanilla until blended. Increase speed to medium and beat until smooth. Beat in additional 1 tsp milk if needed. Drizzle glaze over cooled cake. Cut cake into 24 slices.

Per serving (1 slice): 192 Cal, 4 g Total Fat, 1 g Sat Fat, 152 mg Sod, 37 g Total Carb, 25 g Sugar, 1 g Fib, 2 g Prot.

Apple-ginger mini pies

Prep 25 min   Cook 30 min   Serves 8

5 **5** **5**   (🥕) (🚫)

Use your favorite apples for these adorable little pies. Fujis offer excellent sweetness, as do so many varieties that are at their peak during the fall, including Cortland, Jonagold, and Honeycrisp.

10	**apples, peeled, cored, and cut into ½-inch chunks (about 8 cups total)**
2	**tbsp minced crystallized ginger**
1	**tbsp lemon juice**
1	**tbsp light-brown sugar**
6	**tsp all-purpose flour, divided**
1	**(7-oz) refrigerated pie crust, store-bought or homemade**
2	**large egg whites, beaten**
1	**tbsp confectioners' sugar**

1 Preheat oven to 375°F.

2 In a large bowl, toss together apples, ginger, lemon juice, brown sugar, and 5 tsp flour; evenly divide between 8 (8-oz) ramekins.

3 Lightly dust a rolling pin and work surface with remaining 1 tsp flour. Roll dough out to about ⅛-inch thick. Using a sharp knife or pizza cutter, cut dough into ¼-inch-wide strips; then cut strips into 4-inch lengths (you'll have 64 strips of dough).

4 Using 8 strips of dough for each mini-pie, create a crisscross pattern across the top of each ramekin. Gently press ends of the dough strips onto the rims of the ramekin.

5 Lightly brush dough with beaten egg whites. Bake until dough is golden brown and fruit is bubbling and just tender, about 30 minutes. Sprinkle with confectioners' sugar before serving.

Per serving (1 mini pie): 250 Cal, 7 g Total Fat, 2 g Sat Fat, 116 mg Sod, 48 g Total Carb, 27 g Sugar, 6 g Fib, 2 g Prot.

Cooking tip
If the crusts brown too quickly while baking, cover them loosely with foil.

Apple streusel crostata

Prep 20 min Cook 55 min Serves 12

8 8 8

Use a variety of apples to give the crostata more complex flavor. Try any combination of Granny Smith, Golden Delicious, Pink Lady, Honeycrisp, Rome, or Cortland.

⅓ **cup plus 1 tbsp all-purpose flour, divided**

1 **tbsp unsalted butter, cut into small pieces**

⅓ **cup packed brown sugar**

¼ **cup old-fashioned rolled oats**

1 **tbsp canola oil**

¾ **tsp ground cinnamon**

4 **large apples, peeled, cored, and sliced**

⅓ **cup dried tart cherries**

¼ **cup granulated sugar**

1 **refrigerated pie crust (from a 14.1-oz package of 2 crusts)**

1 Preheat oven to 375°F. Line a large baking sheet with parchment paper.

2 To make the streusel: In a small bowl, use your fingers to rub together ⅓ cup flour and butter until small crumbs form. Stir in brown sugar, oats, oil, and cinnamon. Set aside.

3 In a large bowl, combine apples, cherries, granulated sugar, and remaining 1 tbsp flour; toss to coat. Unroll crust onto prepared baking sheet. Mound apple mixture on crust, leaving 1½-inch border. Sprinkle streusel evenly over apple mixture. Fold rim of crust over to partially cover filling, pleating and pressing lightly.

4 Bake crostata until apples are tender when pierced with tip of small knife, 50 to 55 minutes. Cool 10 minutes on baking sheet set on a wire rack. Slide tart on parchment paper onto rack to cool completely. Cut into 12 wedges.

Per serving (1 wedge): 219 Cal, 7 g Total Fat, 3 g Sat Fat, 81 mg Sod, 39 g Total Carb, 22 g Sugar, 3 g Fib, 2 g Prot.

Winter

Gruyère and spinach breakfast rolls

Prep 20 min   Cook 30 min   Serves 8

(5) (5) (5)   (⌾) (⊗)

Sauté the tomato with the scallion to remove most of the moisture and help keep the rolls from getting soggy.

Nonstick spray

1   tbsp olive oil

5   scallions, green and white parts, chopped

2   large plum tomatoes, diced

1   tbsp chopped fresh sage (or ¾ tsp dried sage)

4½ cups baby spinach

1   (8-oz) tube refrigerated reduced-fat crescent-roll dough

½   cup (2 oz) shredded Gruyère

¼   tsp black pepper (or to taste)

½   tsp kosher salt (or to taste)

1 Preheat oven to 375°F. Coat the bottom and sides of an 8-inch round cake pan with nonstick spray.

2 In a large skillet, heat oil over medium-high heat. Add scallions; cook, stirring frequently, until softened, about 3 minutes. Add tomatoes and sage to skillet; cook until tomatoes are soft, stirring occasionally, 3 to 4 minutes. Add spinach and cook, stirring, until spinach just wilts, 1 to 2 minutes. Remove mixture from pan; cool slightly.

3 Unroll dough; separate it into 2 long rectangles and place side by side. Lift the edge of one rectangle and place it just slightly over the other, so it overlaps the other rectangle by ½ inch; press seams together to seal.

4 Over top of dough, arrange spinach mixture; sprinkle with cheese and pepper. Starting at one long edge, roll up dough jelly-roll fashion; pinch seam to seal. Cut crosswise into 8 slices. Arrange slices, cut sides up, in prepared pan; sprinkle tops with salt.

5 Bake until puffed and well browned, about 20 minutes.

Per serving (1 roll): 156 Cal, 9 g Total Fat, 3 g Sat Fat, 406 mg Sod, 15 g Total Carb, 3 g Sugar, 1 g Fib, 5 g Prot.

Orange-pomegranate buttermilk waffles

Prep 10 min Cook 16 min Serves 8

(9) (8) (8)   (symbols)

These waffles deliver unbeatable flavor thanks to orange zest in the batter and sliced orange segments on top.

Nonstick spray

2   **cups white whole-wheat flour**

½   **cup honey-toasted wheat germ**

3   **tbsp sugar**

1½   **tsp baking powder**

½   **tsp baking soda**

½   **tsp salt**

2   **cups low-fat buttermilk**

2   **large eggs, beaten**

1   **tbsp canola oil**

2   **tsp grated orange zest**

1   **tsp vanilla extract**

2   **large oranges, cut into segments**

1   **cup pomegranate seeds**

¼   **cup maple syrup, warmed**

1 Spray a Belgian waffle maker with nonstick spray. Preheat according to manufacturer's instructions.

2 In a large bowl, whisk together flour, wheat germ, sugar, baking powder, baking soda, and salt. In a medium bowl, whisk together buttermilk, eggs, oil, orange zest, and vanilla. Add buttermilk mixture to flour mixture and stir until moistened.

3 Scoop 1⅓ cups batter into waffle maker to make 2 (4½-inch) square waffles; lightly spread batter to fill each grid. Close lid and bake until waffles are golden brown, about 4 minutes. Transfer waffles to a platter and keep warm. Repeat with remaining batter, spraying waffle maker with nonstick spray between batches, making total of 8 waffles.

4 With a sharp knife, cut off slice from top and bottom of oranges. Stand fruit upright and cut off peel and pith, cutting from top to bottom, turning as you go. Cut oranges crosswise into ½-inch rounds; cut rounds in half.

5 Top waffles evenly with oranges and pomegranate seeds. Serve with maple syrup.

Per serving (1 waffle with ¼ cup orange segments, 2 tbsp pomegranate seeds, and ½ tbsp maple syrup): 283 Cal, 5 g Total Fat, 1 g Sat Fat, 424 mg Sod, 49 g Total Carb, 25 g Sugar, 3 g Fib, 10 g Prot.

Prep ahead

To prepare a pomegranate, cut a slice off the top, then cut the fruit into 4 wedges. Place one wedge at a time into a large bowl of cool water. Holding the wedge underwater, use your fingers to gently remove the arils (seeds). Discard the peel and pith and drain off the water. Pat the seeds dry.

Fig and blue cheese crostini

Prep 15 min   Cook 15 min   Serves 16

② ② ②   🥕

Fresh figs pair perfectly with blue cheese and walnuts. If you don't love blue cheese, goat cheese would work well, too.

Nonstick spray

1   **(4-ounce) piece French baguette, cut into 16 slices**

6   **tbsp balsamic vinegar**

1½   **tbsp honey**

5   **tbsp plus 1 tsp crumbled blue cheese**

1   **cup baby arugula**

4   **figs, cut into quarters**

2   **tbsp chopped toasted walnuts**

1   Preheat oven to 325°F. Spray a baking sheet with nonstick spray.

2   Place bread on prepared baking sheet and lightly spray with nonstick spray; bake until lightly browned and crisp, 10 to 13 minutes.

3   Meanwhile, put vinegar in a large nonstick skillet and bring to a boil over medium-high heat. Reduce heat to low; simmer, stirring occasionally, until mixture thickens slightly and is reduced to about 2¼ tbsp, about 2 minutes. Remove from heat; stir in honey.

4   To assemble crostini, spread each piece of toast with 1 tsp blue cheese; top with 2 arugula leaves and 1 fig quarter. Drizzle evenly with balsamic-honey mixture; sprinkle each with ½ tsp walnuts.

Per serving (1 crostini): 57 Cal, 2 g Total Fat, 1 g Sat Fat, 77 mg Sod, 9 g Total Carb, 5 g Sugar, 1 g Fib, 2 g Prot.

Prep ahead
The crostini can be made 2 days ahead and stored in an airtight container. The balsamic-honey mixture can be made several hours ahead, cooled, covered, and kept at room temperature.

Beef nachos

Prep 12 min   Cook 11 min   Serves 8

3 3 3

Cheesy and shareable–this is the best kind of sports-party food. Add extra jalapeños, chopped cilantro, or a drizzle of lime juice for even more flavor.

Nonstick spray

32 **low-fat baked tortilla chips**

6 **oz (93% lean) ground beef**

½ **tsp dried oregano**

½ **tsp salt (or to taste)**

¾ **cup canned diced tomatoes with adobo**

½ **cup WW Reduced Fat Mexican Blend Shredded Cheese**

⅔ **cup canned refried beans**

½ **cup thinly sliced scallions**

2 **jalapeño peppers, finely chopped (or to taste)**

1 Preheat broiler to High.

2 Arrange tortilla chips in a single layer on a nonstick baking sheet; set aside.

3 Spray a large nonstick skillet with nonstick spray; warm over medium heat. Add beef and cook until browned, breaking up meat with a wooden spoon, 3 to 4 minutes. Season with oregano and salt; stir in tomatoes and beans. Cook, stirring occasionally, until heated through, 3 to 5 minutes.

4 Spoon beef mixture over chips; sprinkle with cheese blend. Broil until cheese melts, 30 seconds to 1 minute. Sprinkle with scallions and jalapeños; serve.

Per serving (4 nachos): 113 Cal, 3 g Total Fat, 1 g Sat Fat, 354 mg Sod, 13 g Total Carb, 1 g Sugar, 2 g Fib, 8 g Prot.

Beef and scallion bites

Prep 12 min   Cook 7 min, plus chilling   Serves 8

① ① ①   ⦸ ⊗

This umami-rich appetizer is based on negimaki, Japanese beef and scallion rolls. Serve these bites as is or with a soy-based dipping sauce.

Nonstick spray

3   **tbsp low-sodium soy sauce**

1   **small garlic clove, minced**

1   **tsp grated ginger**

1   **tsp honey**

¾   **lb lean beef sirloin steak, trimmed and cut into 24 (1-inch) cubes**

8   **scallions, white and light green parts, cut into 24 (1-inch) pieces**

1 In a cup, stir together soy sauce, garlic, ginger, and honey; pour all but 1 tbsp into a zip-close plastic bag or glass bowl. Add beef; press out air and seal bag, then turn to coat beef (or stir beef in bowl, then cover). Refrigerate at least 6 hours or up to 24 hours.

2 Spray a medium nonstick skillet with nonstick spray and set over medium heat. Add scallions and increase heat to high; cook scallions, tossing gently, until light golden in spots but still bright green, about 3 minutes. Transfer scallions to a plate; drizzle with reserved 1 tbsp marinade and set aside.

3 Remove skillet from heat; spray with nonstick spray and set over medium heat. Add beef; discard marinade. Cook beef, turning occasionally, until cooked through and lightly browned on all sides, about 4 minutes.

4 To serve: On each of 24 wooden toothpicks or small skewers, thread 1 piece beef and 1 piece scallion.

Per serving (3 skewers): 66 Cal, 2 g Total Fat, 1 g Sat Fat, 218 mg Sod, 2 g Total Carb, 1 g Sugar, 0 g Fib, 10 g Prot.

Instant Pot® minestrone with pesto

Prep 45 min   Cook 45 min   Serves 8

④ ② ②   ⊘

Be sure to heat the broth before adding it to the Instant Pot. This will cut back on the overall cooking time.

SOUP

- **1** tsp olive oil
- **1** medium onion, finely chopped
- **1** large carrot, sliced lengthwise and sliced into ¼-inch-thick half-moons
- **1** large celery stalk, cut into ¼-inch-thick slices
- **3** garlic cloves, minced
- **1** tbsp tomato paste
- **8** oz (about 1 ¼ cups) dry cannellini beans, picked over and rinsed
- **1** bay leaf
- **1** thyme sprig
- **6** cups chicken or vegetable broth, heated
- **¼** lb green beans, trimmed and cut into ½-inch pieces
- **2** medium zucchini, halved lengthwise and sliced into ¼-inch-thick half-moons
- **1** (28-oz) can crushed tomatoes
- **¼** tsp salt (or to taste)
- **5** oz baby kale

PESTO

- **2** cups lightly packed basil leaves
- **2** tbsp toasted pine nuts
- **1** small garlic clove, chopped
- **¼** tsp salt
- **1** tbsp extra-virgin olive oil
- **2** tbsp grated Parmesan

1 To make soup: Turn on the Sauté function of a 6-qt or larger Instant Pot; add oil. When oil is hot, add onion, carrot, and celery; cook, stirring, until softened, about 3 minutes. Add garlic and tomato paste; cook, stirring a few times, 30 seconds more. Turn off Instant Pot.

2 Add dried beans, bay leaf, thyme, and hot broth. Close the pot and seal the vent; set to High Pressure for 35 minutes. (It may take as long as 20 minutes to reach full pressure.)

3 When Instant Pot beeps, release the pressure manually. Stir in green beans, zucchini, tomatoes, and salt. Add kale, pressing gently to submerge, but don't stir. Reseal Instant Pot; cook for another 10 minutes on High Pressure.

4 Meanwhile, to make pesto: In a food processor, pulse basil, pine nuts, garlic, and salt until finely chopped. With the motor running, drizzle in oil and 1 tbsp water; process until mixture is smooth. Stir in Parmesan.

5 When Instant Pot beeps, wait 5 to 10 minutes, then release remaining pressure. Discard bay leaf and thyme sprig before serving. Serve soup topped with pesto.

Per serving (1½ cups soup and 2 tsp pesto): 191 Cal, 5 g Total Fat, 1 g Sat Fat, 996 mg Sod, 29 g Total Carb, 7 g Sugar, 8 g Fib, 11 g Prot.

Cauliflower-crust pizza with feta, peppers, and olives

Prep 20 min Cook 35 min Serves 4

7 6 6

Rice-like granules of cauliflower make a tender crust. We went Greek with the seasonings and toppings, but tomatoes, part-skim mozzarella, and reduced-fat pesto would be our second choice.

Nonstick spray

½ **large head cauliflower, cut into florets (about 2 cups)**

½ **cup shredded part-skim mozzarella**

⅔ **cup all-purpose flour**

2 **large eggs**

1 **tsp minced oregano**

½ **tsp kosher salt**

½ **tsp granulated garlic**

⅛ **tsp black pepper**

1 **cup roasted red peppers (packed in water), rinsed, patted dry, and chopped**

⅔ **cup crumbled feta**

10 **Kalamata olives, pitted and chopped**

2 **tbsp chopped scallion**

1 **tbsp chopped oregano**

1 Preheat oven to 450°F. Line a large rimmed baking sheet with parchment paper; coat with nonstick spray.

2 Place cauliflower florets in a food processor; process to consistency of rice. Spoon into a large bowl; add mozzarella, flour, eggs, minced oregano, salt, garlic, and black pepper. Spoon crust mixture into 2 (8-inch) circles on prepared pan; smooth with a spoon to form an even layer. Bake until medium brown on bottom, about 20 minutes; carefully flip over. Bake until evenly browned, about 10 minutes more.

3 Sprinkle crust with roasted peppers, feta, olives, scallion, and oregano; bake until heated through, about 5 minutes. Cut each pizza into 4 slices.

Per serving (2 slices): 287 Cal, 12 g Total Fat, 6 g Sat Fat, 926 mg Sod, 34 g Total Carb, 6 g Sugar, 4 g Fib, 15 g Prot.

Cooking tip
Don't worry if you don't have a food processor. You can use a box grater or sharp knife to prep the cauliflower.

Baked beef ziti

Prep 20 min   Cook 50 min   Serves 8

Revisit this saucy, cheesy classic with our lighter version, and you won't be disappointed.

12	oz ziti
2	tsp olive oil
2	garlic cloves, minced
⅓	lb (93% lean) ground beef
1	tsp dried oregano
1	tsp dried thyme
1	tsp dried rosemary
½	tsp salt
½	tsp black pepper
1	(28-oz) can crushed tomatoes
1	cup shredded part-skim mozzarella

1 Preheat oven to 350°F.

2 Cook pasta according to package directions; drain and set aside.

3 Meanwhile, in a medium saucepan over medium heat, warm oil. Add garlic and cook, stirring, 2 minutes. Add beef and cook until browned, breaking up meat with a spoon as it cooks, 3 to 5 minutes; drain off any fat and set pan back over medium heat.

4 Add oregano, thyme, rosemary, salt, and pepper; stir to coat beef. Cook until herbs become fragrant, about 2 minutes. Add tomatoes and bring mixture to a boil; reduce heat and simmer for 5 minutes.

5 In a 4-qt casserole dish, spread just enough beef-tomato mixture over bottom to cover; top with half of cooked ziti. Next, layer with half of remaining beef-tomato sauce and half of mozzarella. Layer with remaining ziti and then top with remaining beef-tomato sauce; sprinkle with remaining mozzarella. Bake until cheese is golden and bubbly, about 30 minutes. Cut into 8 pieces and serve.

Per serving (⅛ of casserole): 253 Cal, 6 g Total Fat, 2 g Sat Fat, 389 mg Sod, 37 g Total Carb, 4 g Sugar, 2 g Fib, 14 g Prot.

Vegetarian lo mein

Prep 15 min   Cook 10 min   Serves 5

(6) (6) (6)   (symbol) (symbol)

Though this veggie-packed lo mein is great any time of year, it's an excellent choice for Chinese New Year. The noodles symbolize longevity, the mushrooms prosperity, and the cilantro compassion.

7	oz spaghetti or fresh Chinese egg noodles
1	tsp dark sesame oil
2	tbsp low-sodium soy sauce
2	tbsp dry sherry
¼	tsp white pepper
1	tbsp peanut or vegetable oil
1	tbsp minced garlic
3	slices ginger, smashed with side of knife
2	cups thinly sliced cremini mushrooms
2	cups bean sprouts
½	cup thinly sliced scallions
¼	cup cilantro sprigs

1 In a 2-qt saucepan, bring 1½ qt water to a boil over high heat. Add noodles and cook according to package directions until al dente. Drain well; return noodles to saucepan and toss with sesame oil. Set aside.

2 In a small bowl, combine soy sauce, sherry, and pepper.

3 Heat a 14-inch flat-bottomed wok or 12-inch skillet over high heat until a bead of water vaporizes within 1 to 2 seconds of contact. Swirl in peanut oil. Add garlic and ginger; stir-fry until fragrant, about 10 seconds. Add mushrooms and stir-fry until mushrooms are just coated in oil, about 15 seconds. Add bean sprouts, scallions, and noodles; swirl in soy-sauce mixture, and stir-fry until noodles are heated through, about 1 minute. Remove from heat and add cilantro.

Per serving (generous ¾ cup): 227 Cal, 5 g Total Fat, 1 g Sat Fat, 214 mg Sod, 38 g Total Carb, 4 g Sugar, 3 g Fib, 8 g Prot.

Shopping tip
Use 100% pure sesame oil, as some brands dilute the sesame flavor by adding a neutral oil.

Lemony one-pan orecchiette with sausage and broccolini

Prep 20 min   Cook 30 min   Serves 6

7 **7** **7**

We've updated this traditional pasta dish with a so-simple one-pot preparation and a welcome dose of lemon.

Nonstick spray

- **1 lb hot (spicy) turkey sausage, casings removed**
- **1 large onion, diced**
- **½ tsp salt**
- **3 large garlic cloves, minced**
- **⅛ tsp red pepper flakes**
- **1 (32-oz) carton chicken broth**
- **8 oz orecchiette**
- **2 cups coarsely chopped broccolini or small broccoli florets**
- **¼ cup grated Parmesan, divided**
- **1 tbsp grated lemon zest**
- **2 tbsp lemon juice**
- **1 cup grape tomatoes, halved**
- **⅓ cup chopped basil**

1 Spray a large soup pot with nonstick spray; set over medium-high heat. Add sausage and cook, stirring often and breaking sausage up with a wooden spoon, until well browned, about 8 minutes; transfer sausage to a bowl and set aside.

2 To soup pot, add onion and salt; cook, stirring often, until onion is softened, 5 to 8 minutes. Add garlic and red pepper flakes; cook, stirring, 1 minute. Add broth and bring to a boil over high heat. Add pasta and cook, stirring frequently, 8 minutes. Add broccolini; cook, stirring occasionally, until pasta is al dente, about 4 minutes longer.

3 Stir in reserved sausage, 3 tbsp Parmesan, and lemon zest and juice; garnish with tomatoes, basil, and remaining 1 tbsp Parmesan.

Per serving (1½ cups): 311 Cal, 8 g Total Fat, 2 g Sat Fat, 1,290 mg Sod, 37 g Total Carb, 4 g Sugar, 3 g Fib, 22 g Prot.

Spaghetti with turkey meatballs

Prep 15 min   Cook 20 min   Serves 1

(10) (7) (7)   ⊗

Here's a super-satisfying dinner to make yourself when there's leftover pasta and you're feeling inspired.

4	**oz (99% lean) ground turkey breast**
1	**large egg, beaten**
1½	**tbsp plain or seasoned bread crumbs**
1	**tbsp chopped parsley, plus more for sprinkling**
Pinch salt	
Pinch black pepper	
Pinch red pepper flakes	
1	**cup hot cooked spaghetti**
½	**cup canned tomato sauce, warmed**
1½	**tbsp grated Parmigiano-Reggiano**

1 Preheat oven to 350°F. Line a small rimmed baking sheet with parchment paper.

2 In a small bowl, stir together turkey, egg, bread crumbs, 1 tbsp parsley, salt, black pepper, and red pepper flakes until mixed well but not overmixed; form into 3 meatballs. Place on prepared baking sheet; bake until cooked through, about 20 minutes.

3 Spoon pasta into a large shallow bowl. Top with meatballs and spoon tomato sauce over top. Sprinkle with cheese and parsley.

Per serving (1 cup pasta, 3 meatballs, ½ cup tomato sauce, and 1½ tbsp cheese): 498 Cal, 11 g Total Fat, 4 g Sat Fat, 1,340 mg Sod, 52 g Total Carb, 6 g Sugar, 5 g Fib, 46 g Prot.

Cauliflower green chili

Prep 40 min   Cook 50 min   Serves 12

Make this chili up to 8 hours ahead and reheat before serving. Tasty toppings include chopped scallions, sliced radishes, shredded lettuce, lime wedges, and hot sauce.

3	jalapeño peppers, 2 green and 1 red
1	tbsp extra-virgin olive oil
1	large onion, chopped
3	poblano peppers, halved, seeded, and chopped
1	tsp kosher salt, divided
¼	tsp black pepper (or to taste), divided
2	tomatillos, husked, rinsed, and diced
6	garlic cloves, minced
4	tbsp chili powder
1½	tbsp ground cumin
1	tsp dried oregano, preferably Mexican
½	tsp ground allspice
6	cups reduced-sodium vegetable broth
1	(15½-ounce) can cannellini (white kidney) beans, rinsed and drained
1	(15-ounce) can white hominy, rinsed and drained
1	head cauliflower
¼	cup chopped cilantro, plus torn leaves for garnish

1 Seed and chop green jalapeños; set aside. Seed and slice red jalapeño for garnish; set aside (leave some seeds in for extra heat, if desired).

2 In a large pot or Dutch oven over medium-high heat, warm oil. Add onion, poblanos, chopped jalapeños, ½ tsp salt, and pinch pepper; cook, stirring frequently, until vegetables begin to soften, about 5 minutes. Add tomatillos and garlic; cook until slightly softened, about 3 minutes.

3 Add chili powder, cumin, oregano, and allspice; cook, stirring, until spices are toasted, about 2 minutes (add a splash of water if mixture begins to stick). Add broth and beans; reduce heat to medium and simmer, stirring occasionally, until slightly thickened, about 10 minutes. Add hominy and cook, stirring occasionally, until chili is slightly thickened, about 15 minutes.

4 Meanwhile, core and trim large stems of cauliflower; on large holes of a box grater, grate florets (you should have about 8 cups).

5 Stir cauliflower into chili; cook 15 minutes then remove from heat. Stir in chopped cilantro; season with salt and remaining pepper. Serve topped with red jalapeño and cilantro leaves.

Per serving (1 cup): 109 Cal, 2 g Total Fat, 0 g Sat Fat, 601 mg Sod, 20 g Total Carb, 5 g Sugar, 5 g Fib, 5 g Prot.

Winter beef stew

Prep 20 min   Cook 2 hr   Serves 4

8 8 8   ⊘ ⊗

Sear the beef first to maximize its flavor, and serve the stew over hearty egg noodles. It tastes even better if you make it a day in advance.

1   tbsp canola oil

1   lb lean sirloin beef, trimmed and cut into ½-inch chunks

1   large onion, cut into ½-inch-thick slices

2   garlic cloves, peeled and crushed with side of large knife

5   tsp red-wine vinegar

1   bay leaf

3   thyme sprigs

½   tsp salt

¼   tsp black pepper

1   cup apple juice or apple cider

1   cup beef broth

2   carrots, thinly sliced

2   cups hot cooked egg noodles

2   tbsp flat-leaf parsley, minced (optional)

1   In a Dutch oven over medium-high heat, warm oil. Add beef and cook, turning occasionally, until browned on all sides, about 6 minutes. Transfer beef to a plate; set aside.

2   Add onion and garlic to Dutch oven. Reduce heat to medium and cook, stirring occasionally, until onion is golden, about 10 minutes. Stir in vinegar, bay leaf, thyme, salt, and pepper. Add apple juice, scraping to loosen any browned bits from bottom of pot. Add broth and bring to a simmer. Return beef and any accumulated juices to pot. Add carrots. Reduce heat and simmer, covered, until beef is fork-tender and carrots are softened, about 1½ hours. Remove and discard bay leaf and thyme sprigs.

3   Divide noodles evenly among 4 plates or large shallow bowls; top evenly with stew and sprinkle with parsley, if desired.

Per serving (1 cup stew and ½ cup noodles): 351 Cal, 9 g Total Fat, 2 g Sat Fat, 610 mg Sod, 35 g Total Carb, 9 g Sugar, 3 g Fib, 31 g Prot.

Thyme and scallion potato pancakes

Prep 25 min   Cook 30 min   Serves 16

These savory, latke-style potato pancakes crisp up perfectly when cooked on parchment paper in a hot oven.

Nonstick spray

1½ **lb potatoes, peeled, grated, and well-drained**

1 **small onion, grated**

4 **scallions, chopped**

6 **tbsp all-purpose flour**

1 **tsp minced thyme**

1 **large egg, beaten**

1 **tsp kosher salt, plus more for sprinkling**

⅛ **tsp black pepper**

1 Preheat oven to 400°F. Line 2 baking sheets with parchment paper.

2 Line a strainer with paper towels; place potatoes and onions in a strainer and press to remove excess moisture.

3 In a large bowl, combine potatoes, onions, scallions, flour, thyme, egg, salt, and pepper; toss gently to combine. Scoop potato mixture into your hands using a ¼-cup measure; press each into a round pancake (about 3 inches in diameter and about ¼-inch thick). Place pancake on prepared baking sheet and repeat with remaining ingredients (you should have about 8 pancakes on each pan); coat pancakes with nonstick spray.

4 Bake pancakes for 10 minutes; remove from oven, flip pancakes, coat with nonstick spray again, and rotate pans in oven. Bake for 10 more minutes and then rotate pans in oven again. Bake until browned, about 10 minutes more. Transfer pancakes to a serving platter; sprinkle lightly with additional kosher salt, if desired.

Per serving (1 pancake): 51 Cal, 0 g Total Fat, 0 g Sat Fat, 128 mg Sod, 10 g Total Carb, 1 g Sugar, 1 g Fib, 2 g Prot.

Shopping tip
Instead of fresh grated potatoes, you can substitute 3½ cups defrosted frozen shredded potatoes if you'd like.

Roasted vegetable and herb stuffing

Prep 35 min   Cook 1 hr 20 min   Serves 10

(4) (4) (4)   (Ⓧ)

We incorporated tons of fresh veggies and herbs into this lightened-up stuffing for a stellar side dish for Thanksgiving or any time.

Nonstick spray

9	**oz sourdough bread, cut into ½-inch dice**
1	**lb peeled and seeded butternut squash, cut into ½-inch dice**
1	**lb Brussels sprouts, quartered if large or halved if small**
2	**apples, preferably Gala, cored and cut into ½-inch dice**
1	**fennel bulb, coarsely chopped**
4	**shallots, sliced**
2	**tbsp olive oil, divided**
½	**tsp salt**
¼	**tsp black pepper**
3	**slices turkey bacon**
1⅔	**cups fat-free chicken broth**
1	**large egg, beaten**
1½	**tsp chopped thyme**
1½	**tsp chopped rosemary**
1½	**tsp chopped sage**
⅓	**cup chopped pecans**
1	**tbsp chopped parsley**

1 Preheat oven to 425°F. Coat a shallow 2½-qt baking dish with nonstick spray; set aside.

2 Place bread on a large rimmed baking sheet and coat with nonstick spray; spread into an even layer and bake until toasted, about 10 minutes.

3 Meanwhile, in a large bowl, toss squash, Brussels sprouts, apples, fennel, shallots, 1 tbsp oil, salt, and pepper until combined; spread in a single layer over 2 large rimmed baking sheets and coat with nonstick spray. Roast until browned and tender, stirring once and switching pans between oven racks halfway through baking, about 25 minutes.

4 Meanwhile, coat a large skillet with nonstick spray and set over medium heat. Add bacon; cook until crisp, turning occasionally, 4 to 5 minutes. Drain bacon slices on paper towels; coarsely chop.

5 Into a large mixing bowl, spoon roasted vegetables; add bread, bacon, remaining 1 tbsp oil, broth, egg, thyme, rosemary, and sage and stir well. Spoon stuffing into prepared baking dish; coat top with nonstick spray. Cover with foil; bake until hot, about 30 minutes. Uncover; sprinkle evenly with pecans. Bake until top is crispy, about 10 minutes more; sprinkle with parsley.

Per serving (¾ cup): 215 Cal, 8 g Total Fat, 1 g Sat Fat, 450 mg Sod, 32 g Total Carb, 9 g Sugar, 6 g Fib, 7 g Prot.

Pecan-spiced sweet potato mash

Prep 10 min   Cook 1 hr, plus cooling   Serves 8

(7) (7) (2)   (icon) (icon)

This starchy side is sweet and spicy. Finely chop the nuts to help evenly spread them throughout the dish.

3	lb sweet potatoes
1½	tbsp packed light-brown sugar
1	tbsp unsalted butter, melted
1	tsp pumpkin pie spice
½	tsp kosher salt
6	tbsp toasted chopped pecans

1 Preheat oven to 425°F.

2 Place potatoes on a baking sheet and roast until soft, about 1 hour; remove from pan and let cool 15 minutes.

3 Slice potatoes in half and scoop flesh into a large bowl; discard skins. Add sugar, butter, pumpkin pie spice, and salt. With a potato masher or large fork, coarsely mash the mixture to combine ingredients; fold in pecans.

Per serving (about ½ cup): 204 Cal, 5 g Total Fat, 1 g Sat Fat, 215 mg Sod, 38 g Total Carb, 10 g Sugar, 6 g Fib, 3 g Prot.

Roasted potatoes, mushrooms, and herbs

Prep 15 min   Cook 35 min   Serves 8

Cut the mushrooms into thick slices or quarter them for the best texture in this ultrasimple side dish.

12   oz baby potatoes, quartered

12   oz cremini mushrooms, sliced

½   cup diced red onion

1   tbsp olive oil

1   tbsp kosher salt

⅛   tsp black pepper (or to taste)

2   tbsp rosemary leaves, divided

2   tbsp chopped parsley

1 Preheat oven to 425°F. Line a baking sheet with parchment paper.

2 In a large bowl, toss together potatoes, mushrooms, and onion; drizzle with oil. Add salt, pepper, and 1 tbsp rosemary; toss well to coat.

3 Spread vegetables in a single layer in prepared pan; roast, stirring once, until potatoes are tender and browned, about 30 to 35 minutes. Toss with parsley and remaining 1 tbsp rosemary before serving.

Per serving (½ cup): 65 Cal, 2 g Total Fat, 0 g Sat Fat, 733 mg Sod, 11 g Total Carb, 2 g Sugar, 2 g Fib, 2 g Prot.

Lemon-sage roast turkey breast

Prep 15 min   Cook 55 min   Serves 8

3 2 2

A roasted boneless turkey breast is a cook's secret weapon—perfect for small holiday tables that don't warrant a whole bird or big ones that need even more meat than one turkey offers.

---

3 **tbsp unsalted butter, softened, divided**

3 **tbsp chopped sage, plus more for garnish (optional)**

1 **tbsp chopped thyme**

½ **tsp grated lemon zest, plus more for garnish (optional)**

½ **tsp kosher salt**

½ **tsp black pepper**

1 **(2-lb) boneless skinless turkey breast**

1½ **cups chicken broth, divided**

6 **large garlic cloves, unpeeled**

2 **tbsp lemon juice**

1 Preheat oven to 400°F.

2 In a small bowl, combine 1½ tbsp butter, sage, thyme, lemon zest, salt, and pepper and mash with a fork; spread butter mixture all over turkey.

3 Place turkey in a small roasting pan or a large ovenproof skillet; pour ¾ cup broth around turkey and add garlic cloves to pan. Roast turkey, uncovered, basting with pan juices and turning garlic cloves twice, until turkey is cooked through and an instant-read thermometer inserted into thickest part of turkey registers 165°F, about 45 minutes. Transfer to a cutting board, cover loosely with foil, and let rest 10 to 15 minutes.

4 Meanwhile, remove garlic from pan; peel cloves. Place roasting pan or skillet with turkey drippings on stovetop over high heat; add garlic cloves, remaining ¾ cup broth, and lemon juice. Bring mixture to a boil, scraping bottom of skillet to incorporate drippings; continue boiling until sauce reduces and thickens slightly, mashing garlic to blend into sauce, 2 to 3 minutes. Remove from heat and strain sauce into a small bowl; swirl in remaining 1½ tbsp butter until melted.

5 Cut turkey into about 24 slices and arrange on a serving platter; drizzle with any juices from cutting board. Spoon sauce over turkey or serve on the side; garnish with more lemon zest and chopped sage, if desired.

Per serving (3 slices turkey and 1 tbsp sauce): 177 Cal, 6 g Total Fat, 3 g Sat Fat, 409 mg Sod, 2 g Total Carb, 0 g Sugar, 0 g Fib, 27 g Prot.

Roasted whole chicken, apples, and sausage

Prep 20 min   Cook 1 hr 10 min   Serves 8

Apples, thyme, and sweet turkey sausage make this chicken dinner as aromatic as it is delicious. Removing the backbone of the bird and flattening it, known as spatchcocking, increases the surface area for excellent browning and decreases the cooking time.

Nonstick spray

2 (5-oz) links uncooked sweet Italian turkey sausage

¼ cup chopped flat-leaf parsley

1 tbsp chopped thyme

2 garlic cloves, minced

1 tsp salt, divided

¾ tsp black pepper, divided

1 (3¼-lb) whole chicken, giblets removed

4 apples, cored and quartered

1 large red onion, cut through root end into 8 wedges

1½ cups apple cider

1 Preheat oven to 425°F. Spray a large roasting pan with nonstick spray.

2 With a fork, prick sausage all over and place it in a medium skillet. Add enough cold water to cover and bring to a boil over high heat. Reduce heat and simmer until sausage is firm, about 5 minutes. Drain, cool slightly, and cut into ½-inch-thick slices.

3 Combine parsley, thyme, garlic, ¾ tsp salt, and ½ tsp pepper in a small bowl. Place chicken, breast side down, on a cutting board. Using kitchen shears or a knife, cut through ribs on each side of backbone; remove and discard. Turn chicken over and use your hands to flatten chicken. Gently lift skin and spread herb mixture evenly underneath. Place chicken in center of prepared pan. Tuck wing tips under chicken.

4 Around chicken, scatter apples, onion, and sausage. Sprinkle apple mixture with remaining ¼ tsp salt and remaining ¼ tsp pepper; lightly spray with nonstick spray. Roast until an instant-read thermometer inserted into chicken thigh (not touching bone) registers 165°F, 50 to 55 minutes, stirring apple mixture once halfway through roasting time.

5 Transfer chicken and apple mixture to a platter and cover to keep warm. Strain pan juices into a measuring cup. Add cider to roasting pan and set over two burners. Bring to a boil over high heat, scraping browned bits from bottom of pan. Cook, stirring occasionally, until cider is reduced by half, about 6 minutes. Strain cider mixture into measuring cup and skim off visible fat.

6 Carve chicken into 8 pieces and serve with apple mixture and sauce. Remove chicken skin before eating.

Per serving (1 piece chicken, ½ cup apple mixture, and about 2 tbsp sauce): 236 Cal, 6 g Total Fat, 1 g Sat Fat, 580 mg Sod, 21 g Total Carb, 15 g Sugar, 3 g Fib, 26 g Prot.

Beef tenderloin dinner

Prep 25 min   Cook 35 min   Serves 6

8 8 5

This company-worthy, one-pan meal features tender beef, roasted fingerling potatoes and Brussels sprouts, and a creamy horseradish sauce. It doesn't take a lot of effort to prep, roast, or clean up.

Nonstick spray

- ¾   **cup plain low-fat Greek yogurt**
- 3   **tbsp prepared horseradish sauce**
- 2   **tbsp chopped chives**
- 1¼ **tsp Dijon mustard**
- 1½ **tsp kosher salt, divided**
- ⅛   **tsp plus ¼ tsp black pepper, divided**
- ¼   **cup minced rosemary**
- 2   **tbsp extra-virgin olive oil**
- 1   **tbsp minced garlic**
- 1   **tsp grated lemon zest**
- 1½ **lb fingerling potatoes, halved or quartered**
- ¾   **lb Brussels sprouts, halved if small, quartered if large**
- 1½ **lb lean tenderloin beef, trimmed and tied**

1 In a small bowl, combine yogurt, horseradish, chives, mustard, ½ tsp salt, and ⅛ tsp pepper; chill until ready to serve.

2 Preheat oven to 450°F. Line a baking sheet with foil and coat with nonstick spray (or just coat pan with nonstick spray).

3 In a small bowl, combine rosemary, oil, garlic, lemon zest, remaining 1 tsp salt, and remaining ¼ tsp pepper.

4 In a large bowl, place potatoes and Brussels sprouts; add 2 tbsp rosemary mixture and toss to combine. Spread vegetables evenly across prepared baking sheet.

5 Rub remaining rosemary mixture all over beef; nestle beef in center of vegetables on pan. Roast, stirring vegetables once halfway through cooking, until beef reaches an internal temperature of 140°F, 30 to 35 minutes. Remove from oven and let beef rest for several minutes before carving and serving. Cut into 12 slices and serve with potato mixture and horseradish sauce.

Per serving (2 slices beef, 1 cup Brussels sprouts, ¾ cup potatoes, and 2 tbsp sauce): 351 Cal, 12 g Total Fat, 4 g Sat Fat, 633 mg Sod, 28 g Total Carb, 3 g Sugar, 5 g Fib, 33 g Prot.

"Corned beef," cabbage, and red potatoes

Prep 25 min **Cook 55 min** **Serves 4**

6 **6** **3**

This Irish favorite is fantastic made with a lean beef round simmered in a warmly spiced broth.

1   **(1-lb) lean beef round steak, trimmed**

⅛   **tsp salt (or to taste)**

⅛   **plus ½ tsp black pepper (or to taste), divided**

1   **tbsp yellow mustard seeds**

½   **tsp cinnamon**

½   **tsp ground ginger**

½   **tsp ground allspice**

½   **tsp coriander seeds**

½   **tsp ground cloves**

2   **bay leaves**

1   **lb baby red potatoes, halved**

16   **baby or baby-cut carrots**

1   **head green cabbage (about 2 lb), cut into wedges**

1 Season beef all over with salt and ⅛ tsp pepper. Place beef in a large stockpot, and add enough water to cover. Add mustard seeds, cinnamon, ginger, allspice, coriander, cloves, and bay leaves, stirring to coat meat; set pot over high heat and bring to a boil. Reduce heat to medium-low; cover and simmer 40 minutes.

2 Add potatoes, carrots, and cabbage wedges to pot and increase heat to medium-high; return to a boil. Partially cover pot and boil until vegetables and beef are fork-tender, about 10 minutes longer. Drain water from meat and vegetables, reserving 1 cup liquid; discard bay leaves.

3 Thinly slice meat against grain and serve with vegetables. Pour some reserved cooking liquid over each serving.

Per serving (3 oz meat, 1½ cup vegetables, and ¼ cup cooking liquid): 328 Cal, 7 g Total Fat, 3 g Sat Fat, 252 mg Sod, 39 g Total Carb, 12 g Sugar, 11 g Fib, 30 g Prot.

Pumpkin-swirl cheesecake

Prep 25 min Cook 1 hr, plus chilling Serves 12

7 **7** **7**

Create a decorative pattern with cookie crumbs using a store-bought cake stencil or just sprinkle the crumbs evenly around the edge of the cake.

Nonstick spray

- 1 (15-oz) can pumpkin puree
- ¾ cup sugar, divided
- 1½ tsp pumpkin pie spice
- ½ tsp salt
- 4 large eggs, divided
- ¾ cup half-and-half
- 5 oz low-fat cream cheese (Neufchâtel)
- 3 oz regular cream cheese
- ½ tsp vanilla extract
- 6 chocolate wafer cookies, crushed to make crumbs

1 Preheat oven to 350°F. Cut out a 9-inch parchment paper round; place in bottom of a 9-inch springform pan and spray with nonstick spray.

2 To make pumpkin filling: In a large bowl, whisk together pumpkin puree, ½ cup sugar, pumpkin pie spice, and salt. Gently whisk in 3 eggs, one at a time, until blended; whisk in half-and-half. Pour into prepared pan; spread to form an even layer.

3 To make cheesecake filling: In another large bowl, using an electric mixer on medium-high speed, beat both cream cheeses and remaining ¼ cup sugar until smooth; beat in remaining egg and vanilla. Pour over pumpkin layer in pan; with tip of knife, swirl both batters to slightly combine layers and form decorative pattern on top.

4 Bake until filling is set along edge but jiggles slightly in center, about 1 hour 5 minutes. Transfer cake to wire rack and let cool in pan to room temperature.

5 Cover pan with plastic wrap and refrigerate until cheesecake is chilled, at least 3 hours or up to overnight.

6 To serve, run a small thin knife around side of cheesecake to release from pan side; release and remove side of pan. Decorate top of cake with crushed cookies. Cut cake into 12 wedges; lift each piece off parchment.

Per serving (¹⁄₁₂ of cake): 166 Cal, 8 g Total Fat, 4 g Sat Fat, 231 mg Sod, 20 g Total Carb, 17 g Sugar, 1 g Fib, 4 g Prot.

Devil's food cookies

Prep 30 min   Cook 10 min   Serves 60

2 2 2   (icons)

These cakelike cookies are a great addition to your holiday baking lineup. They're great as a little dessert or a snack dunked into coffee, milk, or tea.

Nonstick spray

- **2** cups all-purpose flour
- **1** tsp baking soda
- **¼** tsp salt
- **¾** cup cooked brown lentils, rinsed and drained
- **2** large eggs, yolks and whites separated
- **3½ oz** bittersweet chocolate, melted
- **4** tbsp (½ stick) unsalted butter, softened
- **1** cup granulated sugar
- **2** tsp vanilla extract
- **½** cup low-fat buttermilk
- **1** tbsp confectioners' sugar

1 Preheat oven to 350°F. Spray 2 large baking sheets with nonstick spray or line with parchment paper.

2 In a small bowl, sift flour, baking soda, and salt; set aside.

3 In a blender or food processor, puree lentils with egg yolks until smooth; set aside.

4 In a large bowl, using an electric mixer, cream butter, sugar and vanilla until light and fluffy. With mixer on low speed, add melted chocolate; beat until combined. Add pureed lentils; mix well. Alternately add flour mixture and butter, beginning and ending with flour mixture, beating after each addition (dough will be sticky). Set aside.

5 In a medium bowl, using electric mixer and clean beaters, beat egg whites until soft peaks form when beaters are lifted; with a rubber spatula, fold into batter until no streaks of whites remain (do not overmix).

6 Drop heaping tsp of batter onto prepared cookie sheets, spacing about 1 inch apart. Bake until puffed and set, 8 to 10 minutes. Allow cookies to cool on cookie sheets about 2 minutes; transfer to wire racks to cool completely. Store in an airtight container. Dust with confectioners' sugar just before serving.

Per serving (1 cookie): 50 Cal, 2 g Total Fat, 1 g Sat Fat, 36 mg Sod, 8 g Total Carb, 4 g Sugar, 1 g Fib, 1 g Prot.

Snow-capped chocolate yule log

Prep 1¼ hr   Cook 10 min, plus cooling   Serves 12

Be sure to use Dutch-process cocoa powder, rather than regular cocoa powder, to give the cake a deep, chocolaty flavor.

Nonstick spray

5	**oz semisweet chocolate, chopped, divided**
2	**tbsp brewed coffee or espresso**
¼	**cup all-purpose flour**
¼	**cup unsweetened Dutch-process cocoa powder**
¼	**tsp salt**
5	**large eggs, yolks and whites separated, at room temperature**
⅛	**tsp cream of tartar**
4	**tbsp granulated sugar, divided**
1	**tsp vanilla extract**
2	**tbsp confectioners' sugar**
½	**cup part-skim ricotta**
1½	**cups light natural whipped topping**
5	**vanilla meringue cookies, coarsely crushed**
2	**hard peppermint candies, coarsely crushed**

1 Preheat oven to 375°F. Spray a 15½ x 10 ½ x 1-inch jelly-roll pan with nonstick spray. Line pan with parchment paper, leaving 2-inch overhang on 2 opposite sides; spray paper with nonstick spray.

2 In a small microwavable bowl, combine 4 oz chocolate and coffee. Microwave 20 seconds; stir until smooth. Set aside to cool. In a medium bowl, sift together flour, cocoa powder, and salt; set aside.

3 In a large bowl, using an electric mixer on medium speed, beat egg whites and cream of tartar until foamy. Gradually add 2 tbsp granulated sugar; beat until stiff peaks form when beaters are lifted, 4 minutes. Set aside.

4 In another large bowl, beat egg yolks, remaining 2 tbsp granulated sugar, and vanilla on high speed until mixture is pale yellow, 3 minutes.

5 With a rubber spatula, fold chocolate mixture into egg-yolk mixture just until blended. Fold in ⅓ of beaten egg whites just until no streaks remain; fold in remaining egg whites in two additions. Sift half of flour mixture over chocolate mixture; fold just until blended. Repeat with remaining flour mixture. Spoon batter into prepared pan; spread evenly. Bake until top springs back when lightly touched in center, about 10 minutes.

6 Meanwhile, sift confectioners' sugar over a large clean kitchen towel on work surface: immediately invert hot cake onto towel. Lift off pan; carefully peel off parchment paper. Starting at one long side, gently roll up cake, jelly-roll style, using towel to help. Cool completely on wire rack.

7 While cake cools, puree ricotta in a food processor; transfer to a large bowl and fold in whipped topping.

8 Carefully unroll cake on towel (it's okay if it cracks). Spread ricotta filling over cake, leaving 1-inch border on long side opposite you. Reroll and transfer to serving plate. (You can leave as is or cut a "branch" as we did.)

9 Microwave remaining 1 oz chocolate for 20 seconds; stir until smooth. Drizzle chocolate evenly over cake; sprinkle with crushed cookies and candies. Cut into 12 slices and serve.

Per serving (1 slice): 170 Cal, 8 g Total Fat, 5 g Sat Fat, 96 mg Sod, 23 g Total Carb, 16 g Sugar, 1 g Fib, 5 g Prot.

Gingersnap people

Prep 30 min Cook 10 min, plus chilling Serves 60

③ ③ ③   ⓦ ⊗

These crisp treats are perfect for your holiday cookie swap. Or package some in colorful plastic wrap for a great holiday gift.

Nonstick spray

2 cups plus 1 tbsp all-purpose flour, divided
1 cup whole-wheat flour
2 tsp baking powder
½ tsp baking soda
1 tbsp ground ginger (or to taste)
1½ tsp cinnamon
¼ tsp salt
¼ tsp allspice
8 tbsp (1 stick) butter, softened
1 cup packed dark brown sugar
1 large egg, beaten
½ cup blackstrap molasses
1 tsp vanilla extract
1½ cups confectioners' sugar
2 tsp grated lemon zest
2 tbsp lemon juice (or to taste)

1 In a large bowl, whisk together flours, baking powder, baking soda, ginger, cinnamon, salt, and allspice; set aside.

2 In a large bowl, using an electric mixer on high speed, cream butter and brown sugar until light and fluffy. Add egg, molasses, and vanilla; beat until thoroughly combined. With mixer on low speed, add flour mixture, a little at a time, beating after each addition (dough will be stiff).

3 Divide dough in half and shape each into a rectangle; wrap each in plastic wrap and refrigerate until firm, 1 to 2 hours.

4 Preheat oven to 375°F. Spray 2 nonstick baking sheets with nonstick spray.

5 Unwrap dough and place on a lightly floured surface; let stand until slightly softened, 15 to 20 minutes. Roll dough out to ¼-inch thickness; using a 3-inch gingerbread-man cookie cutter, cut out cookies. Place cookies on prepared cookie sheets. Bake until crisp, 7 to 10 minutes. With a spatula, transfer cookies to a wire racks and let cool completely.

6 Meanwhile, make icing: In a small bowl, stir together confectioners' sugar, and lemon zest and juice until smooth; decorate cookies as desired.

Per serving (1 decorated cookie): 70 Cal, 2 g Total Fat, 1 g Sat Fat, 40 mg Sod, 13 g Total Carb, 8 g Sugar, 0 g Fib, 1 g Prot.

Apricot and pistachio rugelach

Prep 30 min Cook 12 min, plus soaking Serves 24

2 2 2   (icons)

Refrigerated crescent-roll dough makes these cookies a snap to prepare. Pistachios and a bit of Demerara sugar add a great crunch.

½ **cup dried apricots**

1 **strip lemon zest**

1 **tbsp brandy**

1 **(8-oz) package refrigerated crescent-roll dough**

½ **tsp cinnamon**

¼ **cup shelled pistachio nuts, finely chopped**

1 **large egg white, lightly beaten with pinch of salt**

2 **tsp Demerara or turbinado sugar**

1 Bring a small saucepan of water to a boil. Add apricots and lemon zest; cover and remove from heat. Set aside until apricots soften, about 15 minutes. Discard zest and drain apricots, reserving a few tsp water.

2 In a mini food chopper or food processor, combine apricots and brandy; process until smooth, adding a tsp or two reserved water, if necessary, to loosen mixture. Let cool completely.

3 Preheat oven to 375°F. Line a large rimmed baking sheet with parchment paper.

4 Unroll dough onto a large sheet of wax paper. Press perforations and seams together. Cover with second sheet of wax paper. Roll out to a rectangle (about 8 x 16 inches). Spread apricot mixture over dough; sprinkle with cinnamon and top with pistachios. Cut dough in half lengthwise. Cut each half crosswise into 12 strips, making total of 24 strips.

5 Roll each strip of dough up to form a little bundle; arrange on prepared baking sheet. Brush rugelach with egg white and sprinkle with sugar. Bake until golden, about 12 minutes.

Per serving (1 cookie): 50 Cal, 2 g Total Fat, 1 g Sat Fat, 75 mg Sod, 6 g Total Carb, 2 g Sugar, 0 g Fib, 1 g Prot.

Cooking tip
The rugelach can also be shaped into crescents: After topping the dough, cut it into 24 triangles; roll them up starting with wide end, arrange on a baking sheet, and curve the ends in.

Anytime

Banana lovers' flourless pancakes

Prep 16 min   Cook 4 min   Serves 2

④ ① ①   ⦿ ⦸ ⦸ ⦸

Pancakes get a makeover when mashed bananas sub in for the flour and sugar. The result is quick and delicious. Adding the cinnamon and nutmeg is really up to you—it's fine to leave them out and still get great results.

Nonstick spray

2   ripe medium bananas

3   large eggs, beaten

½   tsp vanilla extract

¼   tsp baking powder

⅛   tsp cinnamon

Pinch ground nutmeg

½   cup blueberries

2   tsp confectioners' sugar

1 In a medium bowl, using a fork or potato masher, mash 1½ bananas; slice remaining ½ banana and set aside. Whisk in eggs, vanilla, baking powder, cinnamon, and nutmeg until blended.

2 Spray a large nonstick skillet with nonstick spray and set over medium heat. Spoon 2 tbsp dollops of batter into skillet. (You may need to do this in 2 batches.) Cook until edges of pancakes are set and are golden on bottom, about 1 minute. With a narrow spatula, carefully flip pancakes and cook until golden on second side, about 1 minute longer.

3 Top pancakes with berries and sliced banana; dust with confectioners' sugar.

Per serving (8 pancakes, ⅓ cup fruit, and 1 tsp sugar): 253 Cal, 8 g Total Fat, 3 g Sat Fat, 169 mg Sod, 36 g Total Carb, 21 g Sugar, 4 g Fib, 11 g Prot.

Greek yogurt with warm blueberry sauce

Prep 5 min   Cook 7 min, plus cooling   Serves 6

2 1 1   🥬 🌾 🥛

It's not complicated at all to prepare fresh blueberry sauce, and you can swirl it into plain Greek yogurt for breakfast, a snack, or dessert.

1   **pint (2 cups) blueberries**
2   **tbsp sugar**
½   **tsp grated lemon zest**
½   **tsp lemon juice**
Pinch salt
3   **cups plain fat-free Greek yogurt**

1 In a medium saucepan over medium-high heat, combine blueberries, sugar, and 2 tbsp water; bring to simmer. Reduce heat to medium and maintain simmer, stirring occasionally, until most berries burst and cook down into a sauce, 5 to 7 minutes.

2 Remove saucepan from heat; stir in lemon zest and juice and salt; let cool until warm but not hot. (If not using right away, transfer to a container, cover, and refrigerate until serving. Reheat before serving.)

3 To serve, spoon yogurt evenly into 6 small bowls; top with warm berry sauce and gently swirl sauce into yogurt.

Per serving (½ cup yogurt and ¼ cup sauce): 111 Cal, 1 g Total Fat, 0 g Sat Fat, 89 mg Sod, 15 g Total Carb, 13 g Sugar, 1 g Fib, 12 g Prot.

Shopping tip
Frozen blueberries can be used in place of fresh—especially when they're not in season. Just add a few minutes to the sauce cooking time.

Banana-bread overnight oats

Prep 12 min   Cook 7 hr   Serves 10

(7) (4) (4)   (symbols)

Get all the flavors of homemade banana bread in a breakfast bowl. Serve topped with sliced bananas and berries or any fresh fruit you have on hand.

2   cups steel-cut oats

7½ cups low-fat (1%) milk

4   ripe large bananas, mashed well

1   tbsp cinnamon (or to taste)

3   tbsp light brown sugar

1   tsp vanilla extract

1   tsp kosher salt

¼   tsp ground nutmeg

1 In a 5- or 6-qt slow cooker, combine all ingredients. Cook 6 to 7 hours on Low or 3 to 4 hours on High.

Per serving (⅔ cup): 259 Cal, 4 g Total Fat, 1 g Sat Fat, 274 mg Sod, 46 g Total Carb, 19 g Sugar, 5 g Fib, 11 g Prot.

Chilaquiles bake

Prep 12 min Cook 30 min Serves 4

5 **1** **1**

This classic Mexican dish is comfort food at its best and a great way to use up leftover tortillas. Serve it with a side of refried beans or diced nopalitos (cactus leaves).

Nonstick spray

⅓ **cup canned black beans, rinsed and drained**

1 **(6-inch) corn tortilla, cut in half, stacked, and cut crosswise into strips**

⅓ **cup shredded reduced-fat Pepper Jack cheese**

6 **large eggs**

⅓ **plus ¼ cup fat-free salsa verde, divided**

1 Preheat oven to 350°F. Spray 4 (6-ounce) ramekins or custard cups with nonstick spray.

2 Divide beans, tortilla strips, and Pepper Jack evenly among prepared ramekins. In a medium bowl, lightly beat eggs. Stir in ⅓ cup salsa. Pour egg mixture evenly into cups and place on a small rimmed baking sheet. Bake until eggs are just set in center, about 30 minutes. Serve with remaining ¼ cup salsa.

Per serving (1 custard cup): 180 Cal, 9 g Total Fat,4 g Sat Fat, 414 mg Sod, 10 g Total Carb, 2 g Sugar, 2 g Fib, 14 g Prot.

Cheesy kale crisps

Prep 12 min   Cook 20 min   Serves 8

Making kale chips at home is easy and much less expensive than buying them. Store the chips in an airtight container up to several days, though chances are they won't last that long!

Nonstick spray

2   **bunches kale, tough stems removed and leaves torn into 2-inch pieces**

4   **tsp canola oil**

1   **tsp garlic powder**

½   **tsp onion powder**

½   **tsp kosher salt**

3   **tbsp grated Romano**

1 Preheat oven to 350°F. Spray two large wire racks (that you'll set into two large baking sheets) with nonstick spray. The racks help the hot air circulate around the kale and make it as crisp as possible.

2 In a very large bowl, drizzle kale with oil and toss until coated evenly. Sprinkle with garlic powder, onion powder, and salt; toss until mixed well.

3 Spread kale on prepared baking sheets to form single layer. Bake until crisp, about 20 minutes. Let cool slightly; sprinkle with Romano.

Per serving (1¼ cups): 53 Cal, 4 g Total Fat,1 g Sat Fat, 190 mg Sod, 3 g Total Carb, 1 g Sugar, 3 g Fib, 3 g Prot.

Spicy Spanish romesco dip

Prep 12 min   Cook 15 min, plus cooling   Serves 16

2 2 2   🥕 🌱 🚫

The dish's rich texture comes from almonds and a little oil. It pairs perfectly with crudité and chips.

Nonstick spray

3	red bell peppers, quartered
2	tomatoes, halved and seeded
4	garlic cloves, peeled
¾	cup (1½ oz) cubed French baguette
⅓	cup whole blanched almonds
¼	cup good-quality olive oil
1	tbsp sherry vinegar
1¼	tsp hot paprika
1	tsp kosher salt

1 Preheat broiler to High. Line a large baking sheet with foil; spray with nonstick spray.

2 Place peppers and tomatoes in middle of foil; place garlic along edge of foil (as far away from broiler heat as possible). Broil 10 minutes, turning garlic once so it does not burn; transfer garlic to cup and set aside. Broil peppers and tomatoes until skins are blistered, about 5 minutes more.

3 Lift foil up and around roasted vegetables to enclose. Transfer foil packet to work surface and let stand about 10 minutes. When peppers and tomatoes are cool enough to handle, slip off and discard skins.

4 In a food processor, combine peppers, tomatoes, garlic, bread cubes, almonds, oil, vinegar, paprika, and salt; process until completely smooth. Serve at room temperature or chilled.

Per serving (2 tbsp): 66 Cal, 5 g Total Fat, 1 g Sat Fat, 139 mg Sod, 4 g Total Carb, 2 g Sugar, 1 g Fib, 1 g Prot.

Prep ahead
This dip can be made up to 3 days in advance—perfect for easy pre-party prep!

Cheddar potato "fries"

Prep 5 min   Cook 45 min   Serves 4

(3) (3) (1)   (symbols)

Crisp on the outside and tender on the inside—that's the key to great fries. Keep the potatoes separated on the baking sheet so the oven's heat can circulate and touch every inch of them.

Nonstick spray

2   (9-oz) russet (baking) potatoes

¼   tsp salt

¼   tsp black pepper

½   cup shredded reduced-fat (50%) sharp cheddar

1 Preheat oven to 400°F. Line a large rimmed baking sheet with a silicone baking mat or parchment paper.

2 Peel potatoes and cut into ¼-inch-thick sticks (you will have about 52 in total). Put on prepared baking sheet. Spray potatoes with nonstick spray and sprinkle with salt and pepper, tossing to coat evenly. Spread potatoes to form an even layer, making sure they do not overlap or touch.

3 Bake potatoes 20 minutes. Turn fries over and spread out to form single layer. Bake until golden brown, about 20 minutes longer. Gather fries together and sprinkle with cheddar. Bake until cheese is melted, about 5 minutes longer. Transfer fries with baking sheet to wire rack and let cool slightly before serving.

Per serving (13 "fries"): 124 Cal, 1 g Total Fat,1 g Sat Fat, 275 mg Sod, 23 g Total Carb, 1 g Sugar, 2 g Fib, 6 g Prot.

Slow cooker shredded-chicken nachos

Prep 25 min Cook 3⅓ hr Serves 6

9 5 5

Cooking the chicken using canned tomatoes with jalapeños gives it even more flavor and heat.

Nonstick spray

- **1 tbsp ground cumin**
- **1½ tsp ancho chile powder**
- **1 tsp dried oregano**
- **½ tsp salt**
- **1¾ lb skinless boneless chicken breasts**
- **1 large bell pepper, cut into 1½-inch pieces**
- **1 (14½-oz) can petite diced tomatoes with jalapeños**
- **1 (15-oz) can black beans, rinsed and drained**
- **6 (6-inch) corn tortillas**
- **1½ cups (6 oz) shredded reduced-fat Mexican-blend shredded cheese**
- **6 tbsp light sour cream**
- **⅓ cup coarsely chopped cilantro**
- **⅓ cup pickled jalapeño slices**
- **1 lime, cut into 6 wedges**

1 In a 5- to 7-qt slow cooker, combine cumin, chile powder, oregano, and salt; add chicken and toss to coat. Place chicken in single layer; top with bell pepper and tomatoes. Cover and cook until chicken is fork-tender and cooked through, about 3 hours on High. With two forks, shred chicken in slow cooker; stir in beans. Turn off slow cooker. Cover and set aside about 20 minutes.

2 Meanwhile, preheat oven to 425°F.

3 Lightly spray both sides of tortillas with nonstick spray, stacking them as you go; cut stack into 6 wedges. On a large rimmed baking sheet, arrange tortilla wedges in even layer; bake until lightly browned and crisp, turning chips over halfway through baking, about 12 minutes. Let cool on baking sheet on wire rack.

4 Preheat broiler to High.

5 Push chips close together; with a slotted spoon, spoon chicken mixture over chips and sprinkle evenly with cheese. Broil 4 inches from heat until cheese melts and mixture is bubbly, about 1 minute. Garnish nachos with sour cream, cilantro, pickled jalapeños. Serve with lime wedges.

Per serving (1 cup chicken mixture and 6 chips): 406 Cal, 12 g Total Fat, 5 g Sat Fat, 965 mg Sod, 32 g Total Carb, 4 g Sugar, 8 g Fib, 44 g Prot.

Baked honey-mustard chicken bites

Prep 20 min   Cook 20 min   Serves 24

2 2 2   ⊘ ⊘

Set out a tray of these at a party and they'll be gone in an instant. Think of them as a tasty, healthy alternative to classic pigs in a blanket.

1   **(8-oz) package refrigerated bread-stick dough**

1   **lb skinless boneless chicken thighs, cut into 24 chunks**

¼   **cup plus 3 tbsp honey mustard**

1½ **tsp low-sodium soy sauce**

2   **tsp minced chives**

1 Preheat oven to 375°F. Line a baking sheet with parchment paper.

2 Unroll dough and cut into 24 strips; place strips horizontally (crosswise) in front of you. Top each strip with one piece of chicken and brush with mustard; roll dough up around chicken (chicken will stick out on ends).

3 Place chicken bites on prepared baking sheet. Bake until dough is golden brown and chicken is cooked through, 15 to 20 minutes. Let cool 5 minutes.

4 Meanwhile, in a small bowl, stir together mustard and soy sauce; sprinkle with chives.

Per serving (1 chicken bite): 55 Cal, 1 g Total Fat,0 g Sat Fat, 122 mg Sod, 6 g Total Carb, 2 g Sugar, 0 g Fib,4 g Prot.

Buffalo chicken fingers

Prep 10 min   Cook 8 min   Serves 4

Amp up or tone down the spiciness of this kid-favorite dish by adjusting the amount of hot sauce you add to the mixture.

Nonstick spray

1¼ **lb skinless boneless chicken breasts**

½ **tsp salt**

½ **tsp paprika**

1 **small garlic clove, minced**

2 **tbsp light butter**

4 **tsp hot pepper sauce, or to taste**

½ **cup light blue cheese dressing**

4 **ribs celery, each cut into 4 sticks**

1 Spray a large nonstick skillet with nonstick spray and warm over medium-high heat.

2 Put chicken on a plate and sprinkle with salt and paprika. Add chicken to skillet and cook, turning occasionally, until lightly browned and cooked through, 5 to 7 minutes. Add garlic; reduce heat to low and cook, stirring, until fragrant, about 30 seconds.

3 Remove skillet from heat; stir in butter and hot sauce until butter melts. Serve chicken with blue cheese dressing and celery on the side.

Per serving (about 4 pieces of chicken, 4 celery sticks, and 2 tbsp of dressing): 288 Cal, 14 g Total Fat, 4 g Sat Fat, 822 mg Sod, 5 g Total Carb, 2 g Sugar, 1 g Fib, 33 g Prot.

Curry-lime chicken salad

Prep 18 min   No cook   Serves 6

When mangoes are in season, you can use them in place of the apple in this recipe. They are buttery-soft with a sweetness that complements the curry and lime.

2   **cups diced cooked skinless boneless chicken breast**

1   **small Fuji apple, peeled, cored, and diced**

½   **cup thinly sliced celery**

¼   **cup minced shallot**

⅓   **cup plain fat-free yogurt**

2   **tbsp minced cilantro**

1   **tsp curry powder**

½   **tsp grated lime zest**

½   **tsp lime juice**

¾   **tsp kosher salt**

1   **tbsp chopped scallion (optional)**

1   In a large bowl, stir together chicken, apple, celery, and shallot. In a small bowl, whisk together yogurt, cilantro, curry powder, lime zest and juice, and salt; spoon over chicken mixture and lightly toss to coat. Sprinkle with scallion, if desired.

Per serving (½ cup): 105 Cal, 2 g Total Fat, 0 g Sat Fat, 288 mg Sod, 6 g Total Carb, 4 g Sugar, 1 g Fib, 16 g Prot.

Warm kale salad with mushrooms and egg

Prep 25 min   Cook 8 min   Serves 4

When the hot veggies hit the kale, they wilt it slightly and make it nice and tender.

Nonstick spray

¼   cup apple-cider vinegar

4   tsp whole-grain mustard

4   tsp olive oil

2   tsp chopped thyme

1¼ tsp salt, divided

¼   tsp plus ⅛ tsp black pepper, divided

1⅓ cups sliced red onion

2   cups sliced cremini mushrooms

8   cups baby kale

3   hard-boiled large eggs, sliced

1 In small bowl, whisk together vinegar, 3 tbsp warm water, mustard, oil, thyme, ¾ tsp salt, and ¼ tsp pepper; set aside.

2 Spray a large nonstick skillet with nonstick spray and set over medium heat. Add onion, mushrooms, ½ tsp salt, and ⅛ tsp pepper; cook, stirring often, until vegetables are slightly softened and beginning to brown, 6 to 8 minutes.

3 Put kale in salad bowl; top with onion mixture and drizzle with dressing. Toss until coated evenly; top with egg slices.

Per serving (2 cups salad with 2 tbsp dressing): 149 Cal, 10 g Total Fat, 2 g Sat Fat, 770 mg Sod, 8 g Total Carb, 3 g Sugar, 3 g Fib, 7 g Prot.

Barbecue-ranch chicken salad

Prep 20 min   Cook 10 min   Serves 4

8 **4** **4**

Make an extra batch of the grilled chicken to use in salads or sandwiches later in the week.

½   **cup canned tomato sauce**

1   **tbsp honey mustard**

1   **tbsp barbecue seasoning blend**

2   **tsp dark brown sugar**

1   **tsp onion powder**

½   **tsp Worcestershire sauce**

4   **(5-oz) skinless boneless chicken breasts**

½   **tsp kosher salt**

¼   **tsp black pepper**

6   **cups chopped romaine lettuce**

2   **cups halved grape tomatoes**

1   **red bell pepper, chopped**

½   **cup canned black beans, rinsed and drained**

½   **cup canned corn kernels, rinsed and drained**

¼   **cup reduced-fat ranch dressing**

¼   **cup crumbled soft goat cheese**

2   **scallions, sliced**

1 In a small bowl, stir together tomato sauce, honey mustard, barbecue seasoning, brown sugar, onion powder, and Worcestershire; set aside.

2 Heat a ridged grill pan over medium-high heat until hot. Sprinkle chicken with salt and black pepper. Place chicken in grill pan and cook, turning once, until almost cooked through, about 6 minutes. Brush chicken with tomato-sauce mixture and cook, turning and brushing with sauce, until cooked through, about 2 minutes longer. Transfer chicken to cutting board and slice.

3 Divide lettuce evenly among 4 plates. Top evenly with tomatoes, bell pepper, black beans, and corn. Top each salad with 1 chicken breast, drizzle evenly with dressing, and sprinkle evenly with goat cheese and scallion.

Per serving (1 salad): 353 Cal, 11 g Total Fat, 4 g Sat Fat, 1,245 mg Sod, 25 g Total Carb, 10 g Sugar, 6 g Fib, 39 g Prot.

Peanut-butter veggie noodles

Prep 30 min   No cook   Serves 4

Swirl together crunchy, colorful vegetables and a bold peanut sauce for a super-satisfying meal. Add some grilled tofu for extra protein.

¼	**cup powdered peanut butter**
1	**lime, juiced**
1	**tbsp agave nectar**
3	**tbsp low-sodium soy sauce**
1	**tsp dark sesame oil**
2	**tbsp rice-wine vinegar**
1	**tbsp grated peeled ginger**
1	**tbsp red chili sauce**

Pinch red pepper flakes

1	**tbsp vegetable oil**
½	**diagonally sliced scallions**
½	**small head red cabbage, shredded**
1	**large zucchini, spiralized**
½	**cup spiralized carrot**
½	**cup spiralized parsnip**
2	**tsp sesame seeds**

1 In a medium bowl, using a fork, stir together powdered peanut butter, lime juice, agave, soy sauce, sesame oil, rice wine vinegar, ginger, chili sauce, red pepper flakes, and vegetable oil until creamy. Set aside.

2 In a serving bowl, combine scallions, cabbage, and spiralized vegetables. Using your hands or tongs, toss until mixed. Add peanut-sauce mixture and toss until coated evenly. Sprinkle with sesame seeds.

Per serving (1¾ cup vegetable mixture and ½ tsp sesame seeds): 148 Cal, 7 g Total Fat, 1 g Sat Fat, 545 mg Sod, 19 g Total Carb, 10 g Sugar, 5 g Fib, 6 g Prot.

Turkey-pepperoni pizzas with 2-ingredient dough

Prep 20 min Cook 25 min Serves 4

7 6 6

Pizza making couldn't be easier, thanks to 2-ingredient dough. Turkey pepperoni is a delicious topping, but a simple margherita pizza with fresh basil would be fantastic, too.

1   **cup plain fat-free Greek yogurt**

1   **cup self-rising flour, plus more for kneading**

1   **cup canned tomato sauce**

¾   **cup shredded part-skim mozzarella**

20   **slices turkey pepperoni**

4   **tbsp grated Parmesan**

2   **tbsp thinly sliced basil**

4   **pinches red pepper flakes (or to taste)**

1 Preheat oven to 375°F. Line a baking sheet with parchment paper.

2 In a large bowl, using a wooden spoon, stir together yogurt and flour until combined. With your hands, knead dough in bowl until smooth, about 2 minutes, adding additional flour, 1 tbsp at a time, if dough is sticky.

3 Place a large piece of parchment paper on a work surface and lightly sprinkle with flour; place dough on paper. With a knife, cut dough into 4 equal pieces. Use a lightly floured rolling pin, roll each piece of dough into 6- to 7-inch oval. Place on prepared baking sheet; bake until dough is beginning to turn lightly golden, about 18 minutes.

4 Remove crusts from oven and top each with ¼ cup sauce, 3 tbsp mozzarella, and 5 slices pepperoni. Return pizzas to oven and bake until crust is cooked through and cheese is melted, about 5 minutes longer. Sprinkle each pizza with 1 tbsp Parmesan, ½ tbsp basil, and pinch red pepper flakes.

Per serving (1 pizza): 265 Cal, 7 g Total Fat, 4 g Sat Fat, 1,134 mg Sod, 30 g Total Carb, 4 g Sugar, 2 g Fib, 20 g Prot.

5-ingredient tomato-cheese pizza

Prep 12 min   Cook 12 min   Serves 8

4 4 4

With an ingredients list that's pared down to the most delicious essentials, you can have oven-fresh pizza in no time.

12 oz refrigerated whole-wheat or multigrain pizza dough, at room temperature

2 tsp yellow cornmeal

½ cup canned tomato sauce

¼ tsp red pepper flakes

1 cup shredded part-skim mozzarella

2 tbsp grated Parmesan

1 Place rack on bottom rung of oven and preheat oven to 500°F.

2 Turn dough onto lightly floured work surface. With a lightly floured rolling pin, roll dough into 12-inch round. Sprinkle a pizza pan or large baking sheet with cornmeal. Transfer dough to prepared pan, gently pulling dough back into 12-inch round. (If dough resists, cover lightly with clean kitchen towel and let rest about 10 minutes.)

3 Spread tomato sauce over dough; sprinkle with red pepper flakes. Top evenly with mozzarella and Parmesan. Bake until crust is golden and cheeses are melted, 12 to 15 minutes.

Per serving (⅛ of pizza): 142 Cal, 4 g Total Fat,2 g Sat Fat, 393 mg Sod, 20 g Total Carb, 1 g Sugar, 3 g Fib, 7 g Prot.

Garlic-cheese cloud bread

Prep 20 min   Cook 25 min   Serves 12

④④④   ⊙ ⊗

If you have more fresh herbs than just parsley, chop some and add a pinch or two when you whisk together the egg yolk and cream cheese.

Nonstick spray

3   large eggs

3   tbsp low-fat cream cheese (Neufchâtel), softened

1½ tsp garlic powder

1½ tsp dried oregano

½   tsp baking powder

2   tbsp butter

12 oz part-skim mozzarella, cut into 12 slices

6   tbsp grated Parmesan

6   tbsp chopped parsley

1 Place oven rack in middle of oven. Preheat oven to 300°F. Line a large baking sheet with parchment paper; lightly spray with nonstick spray.

2 Separate eggs, putting whites in one medium bowl and yolks in another medium bowl.

3 Whisk cream cheese into yolks until smooth. Using an electric mixer on high, beat whites with baking powder until soft peaks form when beaters are lifted. With rubber spatula, gently fold egg-yolk mixture into egg-white mixture. Spoon mixture into 12 even mounds on prepared baking sheet. Bake until lightly browned, 18 to 20 minutes.

4 Turn off oven and preheat broiler to high.

5 To prepare garlic mixture, melt butter in microwave or in a small saucepan; stir in garlic powder and oregano. Brush butter mixture over each bread; top each with 1 slice mozzarella. Broil 5 inches from heat until cheese melts, 1 to 2 minutes; sprinkle each with ½ tbsp Parmesan and ½ tbsp parsley.

Per serving (1 bread): 131 Cal, 9 g Total Fat, 5 g Sat Fat, 290 mg Sod, 2 g Total Carb, 1 g Sugar, 0 g Fib, 10 g Prot.

Tomato-artichoke calzone

Prep 15 min Cook 25 min Serves 8

This calzone is fantastic with artichokes, but it would also taste amazing with roasted red peppers or leftover grilled vegetables.

Nonstick spray

1   **lb frozen pizza dough, thawed**

1   **cup canned tomato sauce**

1⅓ **cups shredded part-skim mozzarella**

¼   **cup grated Parmesan**

1   **(13¾-oz) can artichoke hearts (not oil packed), drained and cut into ¼-inch pieces**

1 Preheat oven to 425°F. Line a large baking sheet with parchment paper.

2 On lightly floured surface, cut dough into 4 equal pieces and shape each into ball. Roll 1 ball of dough into an 11-inch round; transfer to prepared baking sheet.

3 Over half of dough round, spread ¼ cup sauce, ⅓ cup mozzarella, 1 tbsp Parmesan, and ¼ of artichokes, leaving ½-inch boarder. Fold unfilled half of dough over filling; pinch edges of dough with fingers to seal and roll edge up one turn to form rim. Repeat with remaining ingredients to make 3 more calzones.

4 Spray calzones with nonstick spray. Bake until golden brown, 15 to 20 minutes. Cut each calzone in half.

Per serving (½ calzone) 243 Cal, 8 g Total Fat,4 g Sat Fat, 843 mg Sod, 30 g Total Carb, 5 g Sugar, 2 g Fib, 13 g Prot.

Stovetop macaroni and cheese

Prep 5 min   Cook 15 min   Serves 2

8 8 5   (🍷)(🚫)

The sharp flavor of the Mexican cheese blend, plus the creamy texture of the cream cheese spread, makes this easy dish a go-to weeknight meal.

1	**cup whole-wheat pasta shells**
¼	**cup WW Reduced Fat Mexican Blend Shredded Cheese**
2	**tbsp WW Whipped Reduced Fat Cream Cheese Spread**
1	**tsp unsalted butter**
1	**tbsp all-purpose flour**
¾	**cup fat-free milk**
¼	**tsp salt**
⅛	**tsp black pepper**

1 Cook pasta according to package directions, reserving ¼ cup pasta water. Let pasta cool.

2 Meanwhile, in a medium saucepan over medium heat, warm reserved pasta water and butter. When butter melts, stir in flour and whisk until fully incorporated and light brown, about 3 minutes. Add in milk and cheese, whisking constantly until cheese is melted.

3 Add pasta to cheese sauce and stir over low heat until pasta is coated. Remove from heat and let stand for about 5 minutes to thicken before serving.

Per serving (about ¾ cup): 248 Cal, 7 g Total Fat, 4 g Sat Fat, 449 mg Sod, 37 g Total Carb, 5 g Sugar, 4 g Fib, 12 g Prot.

Chicken, broccoli, and tortellini soup

Prep 10 min   Cook 9 min   Serves 1

7 **5** **5**

Shortcut the prep for this soup by using any mix of frozen vegetables you have on hand. There's no need to defrost them, simply add them in with the chicken.

2	**cups chicken broth**
½	**cup sliced carrot**
1	**garlic clove, minced**
½	**cup small broccoli florets**
½	**cup frozen cheese tortellini without sauce**
½	**cup diced cooked skinless boneless chicken breast**
⅓	**cup diced plum tomato**
1½	**tbsp grated Parmesan**
1	**tbsp chopped parsley**

1 In a small saucepan, combine broth, carrot, and garlic and bring to a boil over high heat; stir in broccoli and tortellini. Reduce heat to medium-low; simmer 2 minutes. Add chicken and tomato; simmer until tortellini and broccoli are tender, about 3 minutes. Serve sprinkled with Parmesan and parsley.

Per serving (1 bowl): 373 Cal, 9 g Total Fat, 4 g Sat Fat, 1,616 mg Sod, 38 g Total Carb, 6 g Sugar, 5 g Fib, 38 g Prot.

Slow cooker cheeseburger soup

Prep 15 min   Cook 2 hr 15 min   Serves 8

5 **5** **5**

Here's a slow-cooker, eat-in-a-bowl version of everyone's fast-food favorite. This soup is rich, creamy, gooey, and super-satisfying.

Nonstick spray

1	**medium onion, chopped**
1	**rib celery, chopped**
1	**garlic clove, minced**
1	**lb (93% lean) ground beef**
2	**tbsp all-purpose flour**
3	**cups canned chicken broth, divided**
1	**cup low-fat evaporated milk**
8	**oz reduced-fat cheddar or colby, diced**
½	**tsp paprika**
¼	**tsp salt**
⅛	**tsp black pepper**
24	**baked low-fat tortilla chips, crumbled**

1 Spray a large nonstick skillet with nonstick spray and warm over medium heat about 30 seconds. Add onion, celery, and garlic; cook, stirring, until vegetables are softened, 5 to 10 minutes. Spray a 3- to 5-qt slow cooker with nonstick spray; add vegetables.

2 Add beef to skillet and cook over medium heat, breaking up with a wooden spoon until no longer pink, 5 to 6 minutes. Pour off any pan juices; add beef to slow cooker.

3 In a small cup, whisk together flour and ½ cup of broth until smooth. Add flour mixture to skillet; whisk in remaining 2½ cups broth. Bring to a simmer, scraping up any browned bits in bottom of skillet; pour into slow cooker. Stir in evaporated milk, cheese, paprika, salt, and pepper. Cover slow cooker and cook 2 hours on Low. Serve soup topped with crumbled chips.

Per serving (about ¾ cup soup and 3 tbsp chips): 211 Cal, 7 g Total Fat, 3 g Sat Fat, 750 mg Sod, 13 g Total Carb, 5 g Sugar, 1 g Fib, 22 g Prot.

Cooking tip
If the soup cooks too long, the cheese could separate. If that happens, combine 1 tbsp all-purpose flour and ¼ cup of the soup in a cup; stir until it forms a paste. Stir the flour mixture back into the soup; cover and cook 10 to 15 minutes on Low.

All-American turkey burger with squash fries

Prep 15 min   Cook 15 min   Serves 1

(8) (7) (7)   (⌀) (⊘)

Cut the fries from the squash's long neck, so you can get the proper shape and thickness. Save the bulblike bottom section for another use.

Nonstick spray

4   oz (99% lean) ground turkey breast

2½ tbsp chopped scallion, divided

2   tsp barbecue sauce, divided

Pinch salt

Pinch black pepper

8   oz butternut squash, cut into ½-inch-thick sticks

½   tbsp mayonnaise

1   hamburger bun, toasted

1   large lettuce leaf

2   slices tomato

4   slices kosher dill pickle

1 Preheat oven to 450°F. Spray a small baking sheet with nonstick spray.

2 In a medium bowl, mix together turkey, 2 tbsp scallion, 1 tsp barbecue sauce, and pinch salt; form into ½-inch-thick patty and place on one side of prepared baking sheet. Put squash on other side of pan. Spray squash and burger with nonstick spray; sprinkle with salt and pepper. Roast turning once, until fries are golden and burger is cooked through, about 15 minutes.

3 Meanwhile, in a small cup, combine remaining ½ tbsp scallion, 1 tsp barbecue sauce, and mayonnaise.

4 To serve, layer lettuce, tomato, burger, mayonnaise mixture, and pickles on roll; serve with fries.

Per serving (garnished burger and fries): 450 Cal, 11 g Total Fat, 2 g Sat Fat, 1,308 mg Sod, 58 g Total Carb, 14 g Sugar, 7 g Fib, 35 g Prot.

Sautéed chicken with lemon-caper sauce

Prep 4 min   Cook 15 min   Serves 4

This easy main course comes together in a flash but the tart, lemony, briny sauce tastes like you made a big effort.

¼ cup all-purpose flour

¼ tsp black pepper

4 (5-oz) skinless boneless chicken thighs, trimmed

2 tsp olive oil

1 cup reduced-sodium chicken broth

2 tbsp lemon juice

1½ tbsp capers, drained

1 tbsp chopped parsley

1 On sheet of wax paper, mix together flour and pepper. Coat chicken with flour mixture, shaking off excess.

2 In a large skillet over medium heat, warm oil. Add chicken and cook, turning once, until browned and cooked through, about 10 minutes. Transfer to a plate.

3 Add broth to skillet and bring to a boil, stirring to scrape up browned bits from bottom of pan. Cook until broth is reduced slightly, about 3 minutes. Return chicken to skillet. Reduce heat to low and simmer, covered, until chicken is heated through, about 2 minutes. Stir in lemon juice, capers, and parsley. Divide chicken evenly among 4 plates. Spoon sauce over.

Per serving (1 chicken thigh and 1½ tbsp sauce): 226 Cal, 8 g Total Fat, 2 g Sat Fat, 350 mg Sod, 7 g Total Carb, 0 g Sugar, 0 g Fib, 29 g Prot.

Southern-style oven-fried chicken

Prep 20 min Cook 30 min Serves 4

④ ③ ③

Using buttermilk, a dash of cayenne pepper, and cornflake crumbs for crunch makes this oven-fried spin a new classic.

Nonstick spray

4   (¼-lb) boneless skinless chicken breasts

½   tsp salt, divided (or to taste)

¼   tsp cayenne, divided (or to taste)

⅓   cup all-purpose flour

6   tbsp low-fat buttermilk (3 oz)

½   cup cornflake crumbs

1 Preheat oven to 375°F. Lightly coat a 13 x 8-inch baking dish with nonstick spray; set aside.

2 Season chicken with ¼ tsp salt and ⅛ tsp cayenne pepper; set aside.

3 In a medium bowl, combine flour, remaining ¼ tsp salt, and remaining ⅛ tsp cayenne. Place buttermilk into 1 shallow bowl and cornflakes crumbs into another.

4 Dredge chicken in flour mixture, coating both sides. Next, dip chicken into buttermilk and turn to coat both sides. Last, dredge chicken in cornflake crumbs, pressing to adhere crumbs to both sides.

5 Place coated chicken breasts in prepared baking dish. Bake until chicken is tender and no longer pink in center, 25 to 30 minutes (there is no need to flip the chicken during baking).

Per serving (1 chicken breast): 224 Cal, 3 g Total Fat, 1 g Sat Fat, 478 mg Sod, 18 g Total Carb, 2 g Sugar, 0 g Fib, 28 g Prot.

Sesame chicken and broccoli stir-fry

Prep 10 min   Cook 20 min   Serves 4

④ ③ ③

Skip the takeout and try our stir-fry instead! This easy weeknight supper cooks up quickly, with chicken breasts and broccoli in an umami-rich sauce. Serve as is, over rice, or atop noodles; it's sure to become a family favorite.

3	**tbsp soy sauce**
2	**tbsp ketchup**
4	**tsp dark brown sugar**
2	**tsp sambal oelek**
2	**tsp cornstarch**
2	**tsp dark sesame oil**
1	**tbsp minced garlic (from 2 large cloves)**
1	**tbsp minced peeled ginger**
12	**oz frozen chopped broccoli**
1	**cup reduced-sodium chicken broth**
8	**oz diced cooked chicken breast**
½	**cup sliced scallions**

1 In a small bowl, whisk together soy sauce, ketchup, brown sugar, sambal oelek, and cornstarch; set aside.

2 In a large nonstick skillet or wok over medium heat, warm sesame oil. Add garlic and ginger; cook 1 minute. Add broccoli and toss to coat. Pour chicken broth over broccoli and increase heat; cover and cook until broccoli is crisp-tender, about 5 minutes. Stir in chicken and reserved sauce; simmer until sauce is thickened, about 3 minutes. Garnish with scallions

Per serving (1 cup): 175 Cal, 4 g Total Fat, 1 g Sat Fat, 924 mg Sod, 15 g Total Carb, 8 g Sugar, 3 g Fib, 20 g Prot.

Slow cooker chicken tikka masala

Prep 15 min   Cook 4 hr   Serves 8

Everyone's favorite Indian takeout dish, lightened up and made in a slow cooker! It's so good (and it freezes so well) that you may want to double the recipe.

1   **(28-oz) can crushed tomatoes**
1   **small onion, chopped**
1   **tbsp minced garlic**
1   **tbsp minced peeled ginger**
2   **tbsp garam masala**
1   **tbsp dark brown sugar**
½   **tsp ground cumin**
½   **tsp ground coriander**
2   **lb skinless boneless chicken thighs**
1   **tbsp kosher salt**
½   **cup plain low-fat Greek yogurt**
¼   **cup chopped cilantro (optional)**

1 In a 4- to 6-qt slow cooker, combine all ingredients except yogurt and cilantro. Cover and cook 3 to 4 hours on High or 6 to 8 hours on Low. Stir in yogurt and cilantro, if using.

Per serving (1 cup chicken and sauce): 177 Cal, 5 g Total Fat, 1 g Sat Fat, 978 mg Sod, 8 g Total Carb, 5 g Sugar, 1 g Fib, 25 g Prot.

Cooking tip
Chicken thighs can hold up to a long, slow cook time. They may fall apart, but the dish will be just as delicious.

Eggplant-and-chicken casserole

Prep 25 min   Cook 1¼ hr   Serves 8

(4) (3) (3)   (symbols)

Make this slimmed-down riff on Greek moussaka by using chicken instead of lamb or beef and a tomato sauce in place of bechamel.

Olive-oil nonstick spray

2   **eggplants, peeled and cut length-wise into ¼-inch-thick slices**

1¼   **tsp salt, divided**

1   **lb (98% lean) ground chicken breast**

1   **medium onion, sliced**

2   **garlic cloves, minced**

2   **tbsp chopped parsley**

½   **tsp dried parsley**

½   **tsp dried chives**

½   **tsp dried tarragon**

¼   **tsp cinnamon**

¼   **tsp ground nutmeg**

½   **tsp salt**

½   **tsp black pepper**

1   **(28-ounce) can diced tomatoes**

2   **tbsp tomato paste**

¾   **cup grated Parmesan (6 oz), divided**

1 Preheat oven to 350°F. Spray a 9 x 13-inch baking dish with nonstick spray.

2 Lay eggplant slices on paper towels and sprinkle with ¾ tsp salt; let stand 20 minutes to draw out moisture.

3 Meanwhile, spray a large nonstick skillet with nonstick spray and set over medium-high heat. Add chicken and cook, breaking it up with a wooden spoon, until browned, about 5 minutes. Add onion and garlic; cook, stirring often, until onion is softened, about 3 minutes longer. Add parsley, dried herbs, cinnamon, nutmeg, remaining ½ tsp salt, and pepper; stir to coat. Cook until fragrant, about 1 minute longer.

4 To skillet, add tomatoes and tomato paste; bring to simmer. Reduce heat to low and simmer, uncovered, until sauce is thickened, about 15 minutes. Remove from heat; transfer chicken mixture to a large bowl and set aside.

5 Spray same skillet with nonstick spray; set over medium-high heat. Wipe salt from eggplant with paper towel and add eggplant to hot skillet. Cook, until golden brown, about 2 minutes per side.

6 Arrange half of eggplant slices on bottom of prepared baking dish, slightly overlapping slices to cover bottom of dish. Top eggplant with chicken mixture and ¼ cup Parmesan. Top with remaining eggplant and remaining ½ cup cheese.

7 Bake until top is golden brown and filling is hot, about 45 minutes. Let stand 10 minutes, cut into 8 pieces, and serve.

Per serving (1 piece): 218 Cal, 7 g Total Fat, 3 g Sat Fat, 957 mg Sod, 17 g Total Carb, 7 g Sugar, 5 g Fib, 21 g Prot.

No-noodle vegetable lasagna

Prep 20 min   Cook 1 hr 10 min   Serves 12

5 **5** **5**

Serve this pared down lasagna with a simple salad. It's a dinner that you can put on repeat.

Nonstick spray

1   **eggplant, cut lengthwise into ¼-inch-thick slices**

2   **large zucchini, cut lengthwise into ¼-inch-thick slices**

12   **oz part-skim ricotta**

1   **large egg, beaten**

¼   **cup thinly sliced basil**

½   **cup grated Parmesan**

4   **cups (32 oz) marinara sauce**

8   **oz shredded part-skim mozzarella**

1 Preheat oven to 400°F. Spray 2 baking sheets with nonstick spray.

2 Place eggplant on one baking sheet and zucchini on other baking sheet; spray vegetables with nonstick spray. Roast 8 minutes; turn vegetables and roast until vegetables are tender but not mushy, 7 to 10 minutes longer. Remove vegetables from oven; reduce temperature to 350°F.

3 Meanwhile, in a medium bowl, stir together ricotta, egg, basil, and ¼ cup Parmesan; set aside.

4 To assemble lasagna, spray an 9 x 13-inch square baking dish with nonstick spray. Spread thin layer of marinara sauce (about ⅓ cup) over bottom of dish. Arrange eggplant over sauce, overlapping slices as needed. Spread half of remaining sauce over eggplant and top with half of ricotta mixture; sprinkle with half of mozzarella. Top with zucchini and spoon remaining sauce over. Top with remaining ricotta mixture and sprinkle with remaining mozzarella and Parmesan.

5 Bake until lasagna begins to bubble, 35 to 40 minutes. Remove from oven and let rest at least 15 minutes before cutting into 12 equal pieces.

Per serving (1 piece): 177 Cal, 9 g Total Fat, 4 g Sat Fat, 573 mg Sod, 13 g Total Carb, 7 g Sugar, 4 g Fib, 12 g Prot.

Salmon with Thai slaw

Prep 20 min Cook 9 min Serves 4

(9) (1) (1)

Savoy cabbage looks like a deeply wrinkled version of the regular green kind. Its ruffled texture helps soak up the slaw's dressing. You could use either type of cabbage in this recipe.

Nonstick spray

4   **(6-oz) farmed salmon fillets**

½   **tsp salt**

1   **tsp grated lime zest**

1   **tbsp lime juice**

1   **tbsp fish sauce**

1   **tsp sugar**

1   **tsp dark sesame oil**

½   **small head savoy cabbage, thinly sliced**

½   **cup shredded carrot**

⅓   **cup chopped cilantro**

⅓   **cup mint leaves**

1   **jalapeño pepper, seeded and minced**

½   **lime, cut into 4 wedges**

1 Sprinkle salmon with salt. Spray a large skillet with nonstick spray and set over medium-high heat. Add salmon, skin-side down, and cook 4 minutes. Turn and cook until lightly browned and just opaque in center, about 4 minutes longer.

2 Meanwhile, to make slaw: In a large bowl, whisk together lime zest and juice, fish sauce, sugar, and sesame oil. Add cabbage, carrot, cilantro, mint, and jalapeño; toss to coat well.

3 Remove and discard skin from salmon. Serve salmon with slaw and lime wedges.

Per serving (1 salmon fillet and 1 cup slaw): 411 Cal, 24 g Total Fat, 5 g Sat Fat, 787 mg Sod, 12 g Total Carb, 5 g Sugar, 5 g Fib, 37 g Prot.

Espresso-glazed chocolate brownies

Prep 25 min   Cook 10 min   Serves 12

(4) (4) (4)   (🔅)

No need to take out the electric mixer! You can make these super-chocolaty, deeply delicious brownies by hand, using a whisk and a rubber scraper.

Nonstick spray

¼   **cup whole-wheat flour**

¼   **cup all-purpose flour**

½   **tsp baking powder**

⅛   **tsp salt**

¾   **tsp instant espresso powder, divided**

3   **tbsp unsweetened Dutch-process cocoa powder**

1   **tbsp vanilla extract**

1   **oz semisweet or bittersweet chocolate**

2   **tbsp canola oil**

3   **tbsp brown sugar**

1   **large egg, beaten**

¼   **cup chopped walnuts (optional)**

¾   **tsp fat-free milk, heated**

2   **tbsp confectioners' sugar**

1 Preheat oven to 350°F. Lightly spray an 8-inch square baking pan with nonstick spray.

2 In a small bowl, whisk together whole-wheat flour, all-purpose flour, baking powder, and salt. In a cup, stir together 3 tbsp boiling water and ¼ tsp espresso powder until espresso is completely dissolved. In a medium bowl, whisk together cocoa, espresso mixture, and vanilla; set aside.

3 In a small microwavable bowl, microwave chocolate on High until melted, about 40 seconds. Whisk in oil until smooth. Whisk in brown sugar until combined. Whisk chocolate mixture into cocoa mixture; whisk in beaten egg until combined. Add flour mixture and walnuts (if using) and stir until just blended.

4 Pour batter into prepared pan. Bake until toothpick inserted into center comes out with a few moist crumbs clinging, 9 to 10 minutes. Let cool completely in pan on wire rack.

5 To make glaze: In a cup, stir together remaining ½ tsp espresso powder and heated milk until espresso is completely dissolved. Add confectioners' sugar and stir until mixture forms a smooth paste. Using a small spoon, drizzle glaze over brownies. Cut into 12 bars.

Per serving (1 brownie): 96 Cal, 5 g Total Fat, 1 g Sat Fat, 51 mg Sod, 11 g Total Carb, 6 g Sugar, 1 g Fib, 2 g Prot.

Cooking tip

If you'd prefer to use an electric mixer, beat together all the ingredients except the flour mixture and walnuts. Then use a wooden spoon to stir them in until just combined.

PB&J cheesecake bars

Prep 10 min   Cook 20 min, plus cooling and chilling   Serves 16

(6) (6) (6)   (🥕)

These rich, creamy bars take no time to make. The PB&J flavor is reminiscent of the childhood sandwich so many of us had for lunch every day.

Nonstick spray

16 **reduced-fat vanilla wafer cookies, divided**

2 **tbsp salted butter, melted**

1 **tsp plus ⅓ cup sugar, divided**

1 **(8-oz) package low-fat cream cheese (Neufchâtel)**

¼ **cup salted creamy peanut butter**

1 **large egg**

1 **tsp vanilla extract**

⅓ **cup blackberry fruit spread**

1 Preheat oven to 350°F. Spray an 8-inch square baking pan with nonstick spray.

2 In a small bowl, crush 15 cookies and stir together with butter and 1 tsp sugar until moistened evenly. Press onto bottom of prepared baking pan, forming an even layer. Bake 6 minutes. Set aside to cool.

3 In a medium bowl, using an electric mixer on medium speed, beat cream cheese and peanut butter until creamy. Add remaining ⅓ cup sugar and egg, beating well. Beat in vanilla.

4 Crush remaining cookie into crumbs. Spread blackberry spread evenly over cooled crust. Pour cream cheese mixture over fruit spread; sprinkle with cookie crumbs. Bake until almost set, about 14 minutes. Let cool 30 minutes on a wire rack. Cover with plastic wrap and chill 1½ hours.

Per serving (1 bar) 126 Cal, 7 g Total Fat, 3 g Sat Fat, 127 mg Sod, 14 g Total Carb, 11 g Sugar, 0 g Fib, 3 g Prot.

Grilled lemon chicken with spring peas, page 50

Recipes by SmartPoints® value

Green

Blue

2 SmartPoints value

Apricot and pistachio rugelach, 223
Baked honey-mustard chicken bites, 242
Cauliflower green chili, 195
Chicken piccata stir-fry, 148
Devil's food cookies, 216
Fig and blue cheese crostini, 176
Instant Pot® minestrone with pesto, 183
Lemon-sage roast turkey breast, 207
Oven-fried paprika chicken cutlets, 151
Pan-fried green tomatoes with remoulade, 62
Perfectly barbecued chicken breasts, 98
Rainbow carrots and sugar snaps, 42
Roasted salmon with chickpeas, 140
Shaved asparagus salad, 22
Spicy Spanish romesco dip, 237
Tomato, feta, and fresh herb tart, 86
Warm kale salad with mushrooms and egg, 249

3 SmartPoints value

5-ingredient tomato-cheese pizza, 257
Beef nachos, 179
Blueberry and Meyer lemon sorbet with thyme, 58
Cheddar potato "fries," 238
Eggplant-and-chicken casserole, 278
Frisée au lardons salad, 17
Gingersnap people, 220
Hawaiian pineapple bowls, 97
Lemony sugar snap pea salad, 21
Open-face egg salad sandwiches, 10
Sesame chicken, 152
Sesame chicken and broccoli stir-fry, 274
Slow cooker chicken tikka masala, 277
Slow cooker red beans and rice, 160
Southern-style oven-fried chicken, 273
Tofu, broccoli, and squash with tahini, 139
Yogurt with rhubarb-raspberry spoon fruit, 53

4 SmartPoints value

Banana-bread overnight oats, 230
Barbecue-ranch chicken salad, 250
Breakfast stuffed peppers, 119
Buffalo chicken fingers, 245
Butternut squash noodles with turkey, 132
Curry grilled-chicken sandwich with mango salsa, 90
Espresso-glazed chocolate brownies, 285
Fettuccine with salmon and asparagus, 25
Garlic-cheese cloud bread, 258
Garlic, rosemary, and lemon oven fries, 143
Greek yogurt fudge pops, 109
Grilled Caesar salad with cherry tomatoes, 78
Lamb chops with balsamic tomatoes, 46
Lemon angel food cake with strawberry-balsamic compote, 57
Lentil, cucumber, and smoked trout salad, 34
Mahi mahi soft tacos, 82

No-mayo pasta e ceci salad, 74
Peanut-butter veggie noodles, 253
Pork tenderloin with watercress salad, 45
Potato salad with feta, olives, and dill, 30
Roasted vegetable and herb stuffing, 200
Roasted whole chicken, apples, and sausage, 208
Salmon with basil-Dijon cream sauce, 41
Slow cooker winter vegetable and farro stew, 159
Whole-wheat chili mac, 163
Zucchini and tomato pita pizzas, 89

5 SmartPoints value

Almond-cherry oat bars, 113
Apple-cider chicken salad, 127
Apple-ginger mini pies, 167
Butternut squash–crust fontina pizza, 131
Chicken, broccoli, and tortellini soup, 265
Chili-rubbed pork chops, 105
Flank steak with tomatoes and basil, 106
Grilled corn, chicken, and vegetable salad, 81
Grilled tuna with cucumber-noodle salad, 38
Gruyère and spinach breakfast rolls, 172
Hearty chicken stew with parsley dumplings, 33
Italian pasta salad with tomatoes and artichokes, 77
No-noodle vegetable lasagna, 281
Roasted chicken, artichokes, and potatoes, 49
Sautéed chicken with lemon-caper sauce, 270
Slow cooker cheeseburger soup, 266
Slow cooker chicken with chile and corn, 101
Slow cooker shredded-chicken nachos, 241
Summer vegetable tart, 85

6 SmartPoints value

Blueberry-peach cornmeal cupcakes, 110
Cauliflower-crust pizza with feta, peppers, and olives, 184
"Corned beef," cabbage, and red potatoes, 212
Grilled cheddar-cheese sandwiches, 128
Orecchiette with roasted Brussels sprouts and grapes, 136
Pan-fried fish sandwich, 37
Pasta and spring vegetables with feta, 26
PB&J cheesecake bars, 286
Pot roast with gravy, 155
Roasted brisket, 156
Turkey-pepperoni pizzas with 2-ingredient dough, 254
Vegetarian lo mein, 188

7 SmartPoints value

All-American turkey burger with squash fries, 269
Baked beef ziti, 187
Irish oatmeal with roasted apples, 120
Lemony one-pan orecchiette with sausage and broccolini, 191
Pecan-spiced sweet potato mash, 203
Pumpkin-swirl cheesecake, 215
Snow-capped chocolate yule log, 219
Spaghetti with turkey meatballs, 192

Purple

Beef and scallion bites,
page 180

Index